I0435057

Climate Change on the Shoshone National Forest, Wyoming:

A Synthesis of Past Climate, Climate Projections, and Ecosystem Implications

Janine Rice, Andrew Tredennick, and Linda A. Joyce

United States Department of Agriculture / Forest Service
Rocky Mountain Research Station
General Technical Report RMRS-GTR-264
January 2012

ABSTRACT

The Shoshone National Forest (Shoshone) covers 2.4 million acres of mountainous topography in northwest Wyoming and is a vital ecosystem that provides clean water, wildlife habitat, timber, grazing, recreational opportunities, and aesthetic value. The Shoshone has experienced and adapted to changes in climate for many millennia, and is currently experiencing a warming trend that is expected to accelerate in the next century. Climate change directly and indirectly affects the Shoshone's high-elevation, mountainous terrain that supports unique and sometimes rare ecological components. Several vulnerable and very responsive resources and processes on the Shoshone could interact to produce unforeseeable or undesirable ecosystem changes, highlighting the need to identify potential resource vulnerabilities and develop adaptation pathways and flexibility in resource management options. The objective of this report is to synthesize the current understanding of the paleo and historical climate of the Shoshone as a reference point, determine what future climates may look like, and what the effects of future climate may be on natural resources. This information allows for the identification of vulnerabilities and information gaps, thereby aiding the development of adaptation tools and strategies.

Keywords: climate change, ecosystem services, vulnerability, resource management, Shoshone National Forest, Greater Yellowstone Ecosytem

AUTHORS

Janine Rice is a Research Associate with the University of Colorado, Western Water Assessment and the U.S. Department of Agriculture Forest Service, Rocky Mountain Research Station, Fort Collins, Colorado.

Andrew Tredennick is a doctoral student at Colorado State University, Fort Collins, Colorado.

Linda A. Joyce is a Quantitative Ecologist with the Human Dimensions Research Program at the U.S. Department of Agriculture Forest Service, Rocky Mountain Research Station, Fort Collins, Colorado.

ACNOWLEDGMENTS

We acknowledge support for this project from the USDA Forest Service, Global Change Research Program, which funded the larger project "A Toolkit for Adapting to Climate Change on Western National Forests: Incorporating Climate into Resource Management and Planning." We also thank several reviewers: Bryan Armel, Greg Bevenger, Ray Zubik, Kent Houston, Claudia Regan, Polly Hays, Cindy Swanson, Tom Olliff, and Virginia Kelly.

Shoshone National Forest

CONTENTS

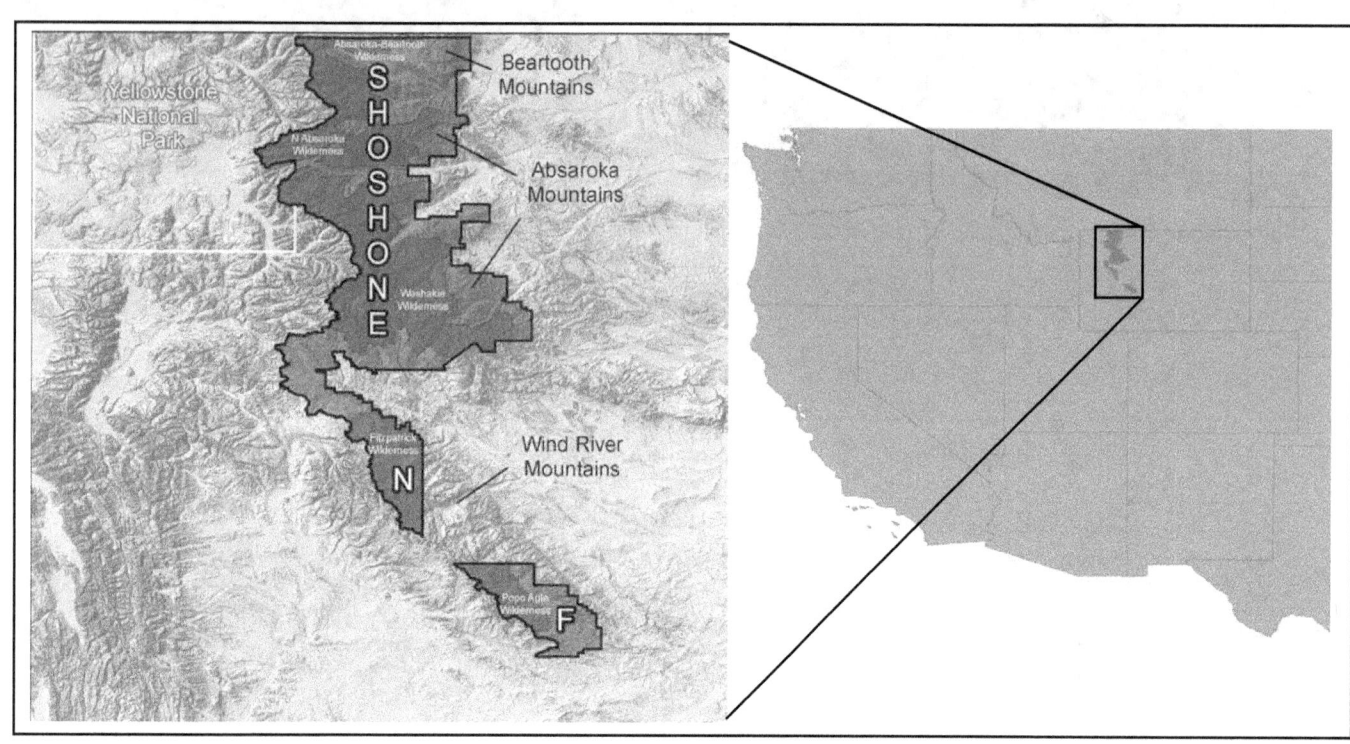

Figure 1. Shoshone National Forest boundary.

Introduction

Climate is defined as the average weather or, more rigorously, as the statistical description in terms of the mean and variability of relevant quantities (for example, temperature, precipitation, snow, and wind) over a period of time ranging from months to thousands or millions of years (IPCC 2007a). From the paleo (prehistoric) records, we know that climate is constantly changing and that these changes prompt ecosystems to adjust (Whitlock 1993; Lyford and others 2003). As a natural process, this reactive adjustment is the adaptation that species and ecosystems make in response to environmental changes. Within human systems, adaptation refers to management actions and decisions that help ecological, social, and economic systems accommodate the challenges imposed or seek opportunities that arise from variations in climate and other disturbances (Joyce and others 2008a).

The effects of climate change on ecosystem structure, function, and benefits humankind receives from natural ecosystem resources and processes (ecosystem services) are functions of the ecological sensitivity to variations in climate, the degree to which the climate changes, and the adaptability of plants and animals (Hassan and others 2005 [Part II: Assessment of Ecosystem Services]; Brown and others 2006; Joyce and others 2008a). While knowledge of regional and local climates and their variations across the landscape is important for resource management decisions, even more important may be an understanding of the vulnerability and the adaptive capacity of plants, animals, and ecosystems facing a changing climate. The information provided in this report helps to identify potential adaptation pathways and flexibility in resource management options.

Climate change introduces a significant challenge for land managers and decision-makers in the western United States, as climate related changes of ecosystems behavior (e.g., glacier melt, snow cover, snowpack, beetle outbreaks, length of growing season, and wildfires) are already being documented (Ryan and others 2008; U.S. EPA 2010). The rapid accumulation of scientific information of the effects of climate change over the last 20 years has been challenging for resource managers to effectively incorporate into on-the-ground management. While much information is available, it is difficult to extrapolate research results from other environments to the landscape of interest to resource managers. Also, many existing paradigms (e.g., historic range of variation) and tools (e.g., planting guidelines) assume long-term climate stability, which may no longer be viable.

East of Yellowstone National Park (YNP) and west of small towns, ranches, irrigated agricultural lands, and the Wind River Indian Reservation, the Shoshone National Forest (Shoshone) in northwest Wyoming provides diverse habitats for plants and animals as well as a variety of ecosystem services (Figure 1). Covering 2.4 million acres (982,982 ha) and elevation gradients spanning from 4599 (1402 m) at Clarks Fork Canyon to 13,845 ft (4221 m) at Gannet Peak, Wyoming's highest peak, the Shoshone is home to alpine meadows, conifer and aspen forests, grasslands, and sagebrush shrublands. Sensitive species such as the Yellowstone cutthroat trout (*Oncorhynchus clarkii bouvieri*) and lynx (*Lynx canadensis*) find habitat on the Shoshone. The diversity of ecosystem services includes domestic livestock grazing, mining, oil and gas leasing, and timber harvest, as well as recreation, tourism, and water for irrigation. The surrounding communities benefit economically from tourism and recreation activities within the Shoshone and the nearby YNP. Opportunities include the first designated Wild and Scenic River, the Clarks Fork of the Yellowstone River, the internationally recognized Continental Divide National Scenic Trail and Nez Perce National Historic Trail, as well as five wilderness areas—North Absaroka, Absaroka-Beartooth, Washakie, Fitzpatrick, and Popo Agie. Water runoff from the Shoshone contributes to hydropower generation at the Buffalo Bill and Shoshone dams, and to irrigation water for agricultural lands to the east. The Shoshone is home to a large concentration of glaciers that occupy high elevations in the Wind River and Absaroka mountain ranges (Krimmel 2002).

The Shoshone's diverse ecosystems and services they provide may experience changes in climate that they may or may not be able to adapt to. Ecosystem services (benefits we receive from ecosystems) that may be vulnerable to climate change include: provisioning services such as water supply and food production, regulating services such as erosion or flood control and carbon (C) storage, cultural services such as recreational benefits, and supporting services such as nutrient cycling that maintain conditions for life on Earth (MEA 2005). The objective of this report is to synthesize the current understanding of the paleo and historical climate of the Shoshone as a reference point, determine what future climates may look like, and what the effects of future climate may be on natural resources. This information allows for the identification of vulnerabilities and information gaps, thereby aiding the development of adaptation tools and strategies. Current scientific information presented in this report draws on the referred and gray literature for studies done within the boundaries of the Shoshone and studies conducted in similar geographic areas, and at larger spatial scales. We draw on studies focusing on the Greater Yellowstone Ecosystem (GYE) (Figure 2) or on the western or entire United States, or on general studies when no Shoshone-specific information is available. However, many of these studies focus on YNP—the differences between the outlying areas and the Shoshone have not been studied in depth. Where existing paradigms and tools have been scrutinized in the light of a changing climate, we report the implications of climate change to these traditional management practices. Where little information is available, we identify needed research.

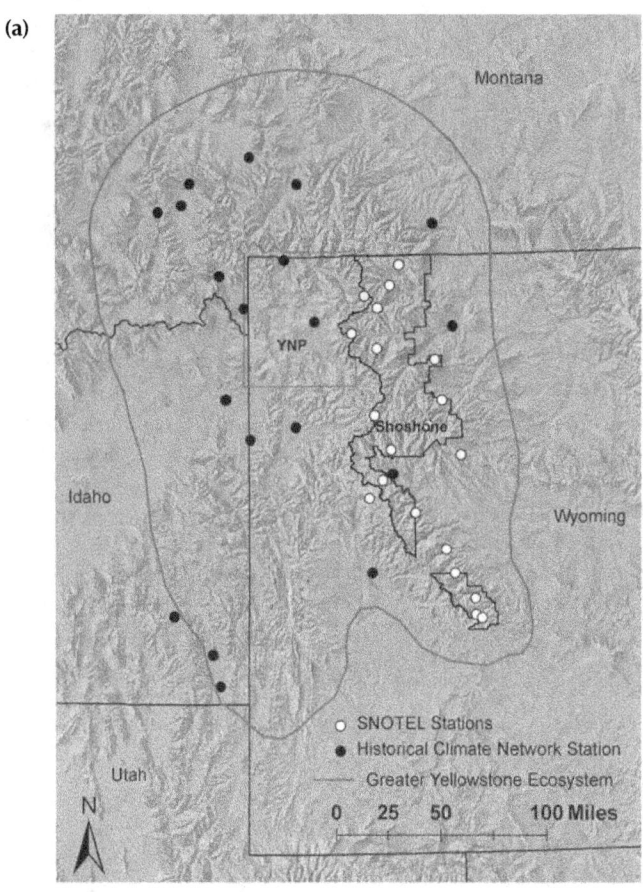

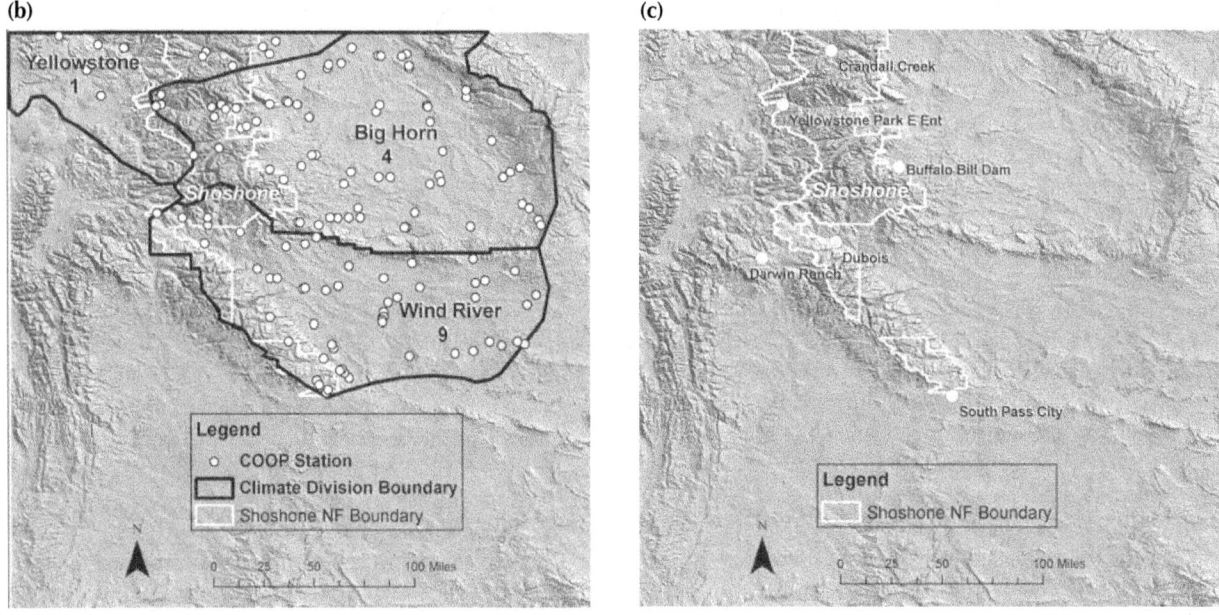

Figure 2. Climate station locations for (a) the Historical Climate Network on the Shoshone and GYE; (b) Climate Divisions 1, 4, and 9; and (c) Climate stations on or near the Shoshone National Forest.

USDA Forest Service RMRS-GTR-264. 2012.

Climate of the Greater Yellowstone Ecosystem and Shoshone National Forest

Scientific research combined with management experience reflects an awareness of the variation in current climate and an understanding of the great variation of climate from 20,000 years before present (BP) to present within the GYE. We summarize current climate and climate of the Twentieth Century for the GYE based on observations. Over this period, management direction within the GYE has evolved based on the experience of managers with climatic events such as droughts and fire. Research studies on climate in the western United States from the Last Glacial Maximum (20,000 BP) to the Twentieth Century has deepened the understanding of climate dynamics and the response of vegetation and ecosystems to changes in climate. We summarize this research where it focused on the GYE and the Shoshone. We compare the variation of the paleoclimate with the historical climate on which current management is based.

Current Climate of the Greater Yellowstone Ecosystem and Shoshone National Forest

Introduction

Although the State of Wyoming has many climate and hydrology networks collecting weather and water data (Curtis and Grimes 2004; Table 2.A), few with complete, long-term records are found within the Shoshone or at high elevations in the GYE. We draw on a variety of published sources and data to describe the current (1971 to 2000) and Twentieth Century historical climate of the GYE and Shoshone. To explore the spatial patterns of climate within the GYE, we use spatially interpolated climate data from the Parameter-Elevation Regressions and Independent Slopes Model (PRISM) at 2625-ft (800-m) grid resolution (Daly and others 2008). Two generalized precipitation regimes have been used to define seasonal precipitation patterns in the GYE (Despain 1987). We use the ratio between summer and winter precipitation to explore these patterns across the GYE.

To establish a basis for comparison of climate over time, we obtained climate data (see below for sources, also Appendix Tables 1 through 3) to compute 30-year averages over the Twentieth Century (1901-1930 to 1971-2000) and explore the variation in this metric over 100 years following Curtis and Grimes (2002). The temporal patterns of

the Twentieth Century climate are explored at three different spatial scales: GYE, climate division within northwest Wyoming, and the Shoshone (Figure 2). To establish the recent historical climate of the GYE, data from 19 Historic Climate Network stations (http://cdiac.ornl.gov/epubs/ndp/ushcn/access html) located in northwest Wyoming, eastern Idaho, and southwest Montana were analyzed (Figure 2a). Three of the 10 climate divisions in the State of Wyoming fall on the Shoshone: the Yellowstone River Drainage (Division 1), the Big Horn River Drainage (Division 4), and the Wind River Drainage (Division 9) (NOAA 2010, http://www.esrl noaa.gov/psd/data/timeseries/). Divisional data have been used to explore large scale anomalies such as droughts and cold winters (Guttman and Quayle 1996). Gray and others (2007) found that the climate records from Division 1 were closely related to the tree growth, as measured in long-term tree ring data in southwestern Montana and northwestern Wyoming (Figure 3). Temporal patterns are examined at the level of these three divisions to contrast with the climate of the GYE (Figure 2b). Finally, 6 climate stations (Western Regional Climate Center 2010; http://www.wrcc.dri.edu/summary/Climsmwy.html) and 20 snowpack telemetry (SNOTEL) stations (NRCS 2010; http://www.wcc nrcs.usda.gov/snotel/Wyoming/wyoming html) that fall within or near the Shoshone are used to identify finer spatial patterns (Figures 2a and 2c). The data available from the six climate stations varies in length from 10 years

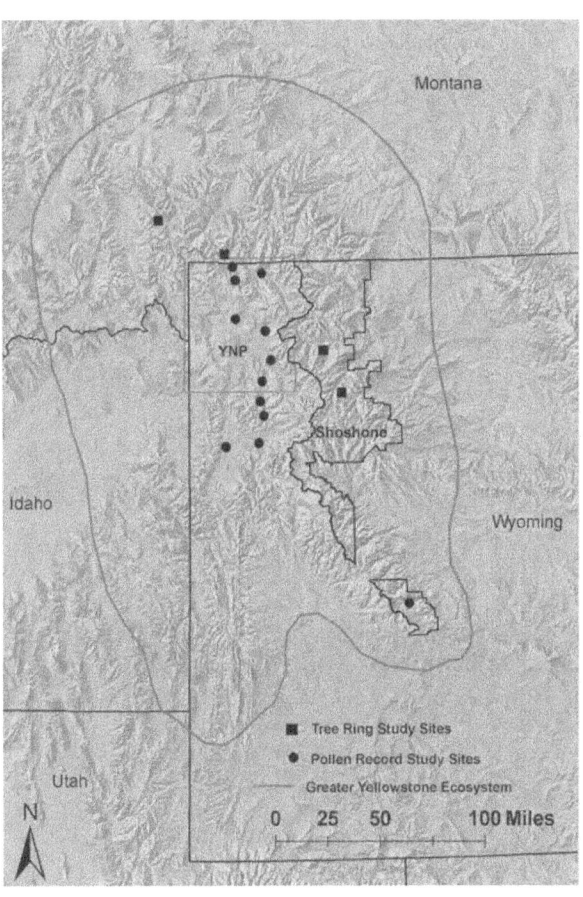

Figure 3. Approximate location for tree ring sites from Gray and others (2006), and pollen record sites from Whitlock and Bartlein (1993), Whitlock (1993), and Huerta and others (2009).

to nearly 100 years; whereas the SNOTEL sites have periods of record of about 30 years (1980s to 2009). Elevations of the climate stations range from 5390 to 8160 ft (1643 to 2489 m), and for the SNOTEL sites from 7120 to 10,100 ft (2170 to 3078 m) (Appendix Table 3).

Spatial Climate Patterns

Spatial patterns of annual temperature and cumulative annual precipitation vary greatly across the GYE region (Figures 4 and 5). The coolest temperatures (<32 °F [0 °C]) were recorded mostly on the Shoshone in the Wind River Mountains, in the Absaroka Mountains, and just to the north of the Shoshone into southern Montana (see Figure 1 for mountain range location and Figure 4 for temperature). Annual precipitation is greatest in the western parts of YNP and just south of this area (Figure 5). Valley bottoms and the high plains are the warmest and driest areas of the GYE, which have a growing season (sum of growing degree days greater than 2500) longer than five months, while upper elevations can have a growing season of two to three months (Hansen 2006). Based on the PRISM data (Daly and others 2008), annual temperatures within the Shoshone range from 47 °F (8 °C) in the lowest elevations to 10 °F (-12 °C) in the highest elevations (Figure 4). Annual precipitation for the Shoshone ranges from 10 inches/year (254 mm/year) in the lowest elevations to 60 inches/year (1525 mm/year) in the highest elevations—much less than the nearly 100 inches (2540 mm) received in other mountain ranges of the GYE (Figure 5). Precipitation in the valleys and plains to the east and south of the Shoshone can be less than 10 inches per year (254 mm/year) (Figure 5).

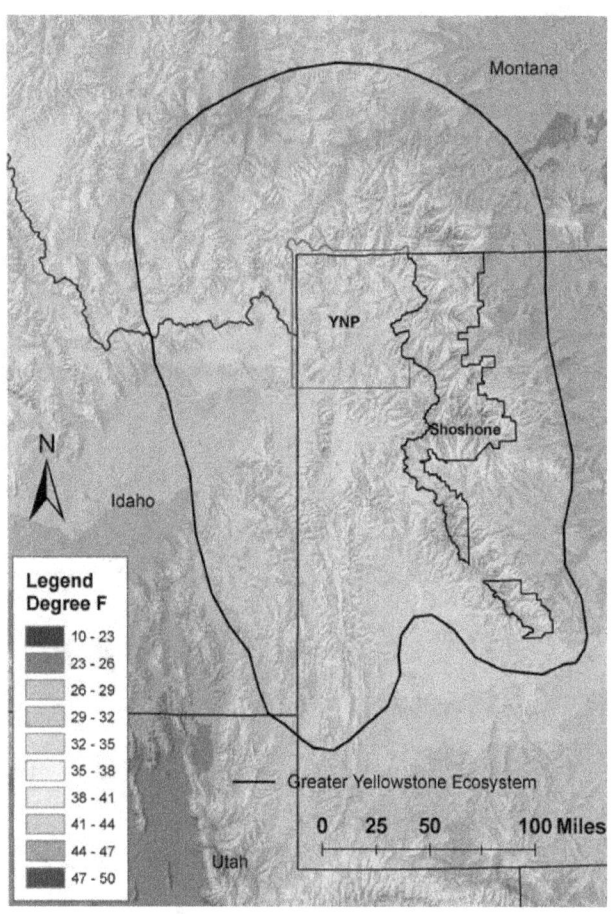

Figure 4. Average temperature (°F) (1971 to 2000).

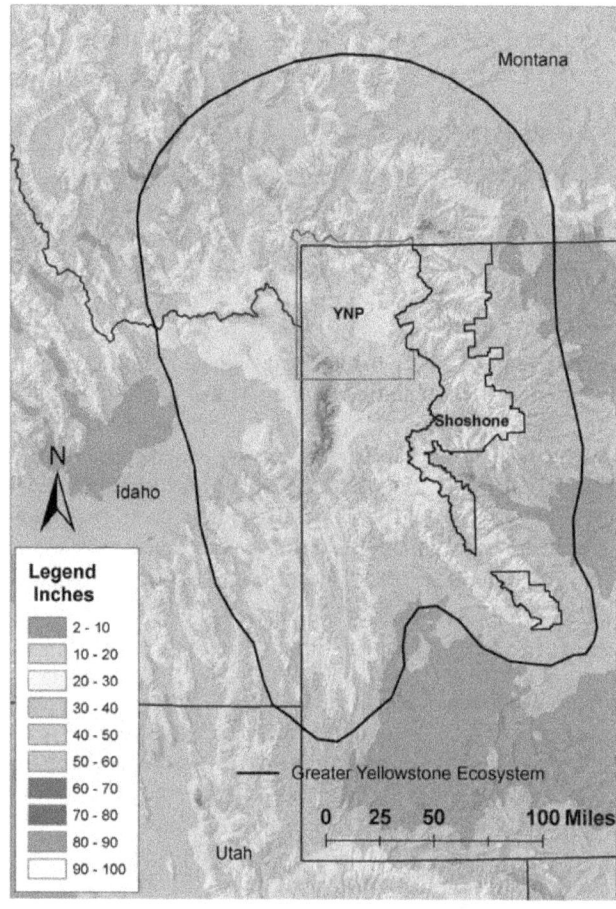

Figure 5. Average precipitation (inches) (1971 to 2000).

USDA Forest Service RMRS-GTR-264. 2012.

Winter-wet and summer-wet precipitation regimes (Figure 6) are a result of the GYE being situated between a transition zone of two major continental air masses in the Southwest and Pacific Northwest that have remained stable for about 9000 years (Despain 1987; Mock 1996; Huerta and others 2009). The summer monsoon cycle from the Gulfs of California and Mexico influences the summer-wet areas of the GYE. Summer-wet areas can be seen in the northern and eastern areas of the GYE, especially at lower elevations (Figure 6, pink areas). The Pacific Northwest experiences high levels of winter precipitation and dry summers that influence the winter-wet areas of the GYE. Winter-wet areas can be seen to the west and south of the GYE, especially at high elevations (Figure 6, blue areas). Winter season is defined as December through February, and summer as June through August.

Shoshone summer-wet, low-elevation areas commonly receive twice as much precipitation during summer as opposed to winter. Some of these low-elevation areas can receive up to four times as much precipitation during summer as opposed to winter. Winter-wet areas can commonly receive twice as much precipitation during winter, and in the highest elevations of the Western Shoshone, up to four times

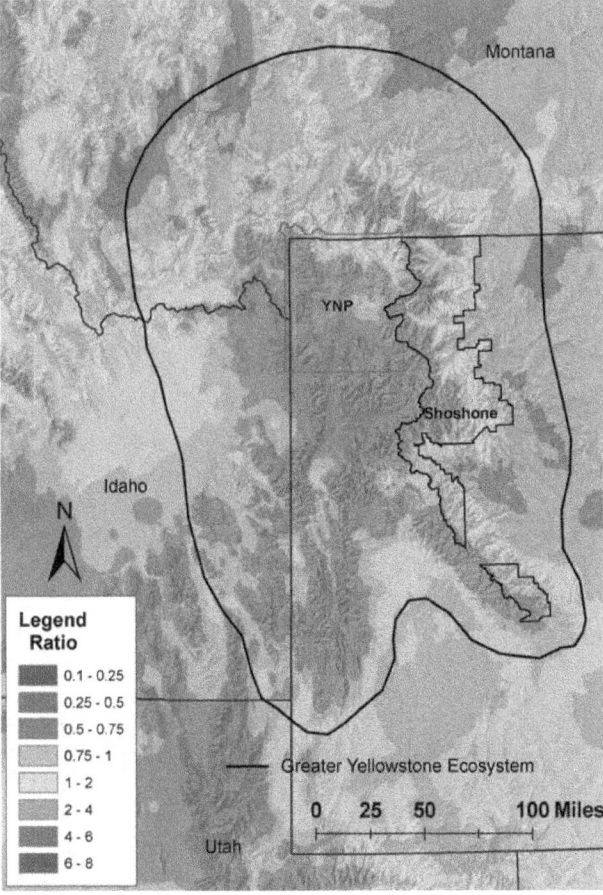

Figure 6. Summer/winter precipitation ratio (1971 to 2000 average).

as much precipitation during winter (Figure 6). Areas west of the Shoshone can receive as much as 4 to 10 times more precipitation during winter compared to summer (Figure 6).

Temporal Climate Patterns

The Greater Yellowstone Ecosystem

Temporal patterns of temperature and precipitation across the GYE show several months with an average temperature less than freezing and monthly precipitation of 1 to 2.5 inches (25.4 to 63.5 mm) (Figure 7). According to data from 19 Historical Climate Network stations within the GYE, annual precipitation averaged around 16 inches (406 mm) (Figure 7a), and annual temperature was just under 40 °F (4.4 °C) (moving average of 30-year periods from 1901 to 2000) (Figure 7b).

The 30-year averages for annual precipitation increased from slightly above 15 inches (381 mm) from 1901 to 1930, to over 18 inches (457 mm) from 1971 to 2000 (Figure 7a). Monthly precipitation is greatest in May and June, and these months also show the greatest variation—nearly 1 inch (25 mm) across all of the 30-year averages. Other months, such as February showed little variation in the 30-year precipitation averages across the 100-year period; however, precipitation for all months except January, June, and December, increased in the second half of the century.

The 30-year averages for annual temperature increased nearly 1 °F (0.6 °C) across the 100-year period (Figure 7b). Monthly temperatures ranged from 17 °F (-8 °C) during January to 63 °F (17 °C) during July. As with precipitation, the monthly 30-year averages varied over the 100 years. The greatest variation (more than 2 °F [1.1 °C]) was seen in February and March. June through August 30-year averages varied less than 1 °F (0.6 °C). A decrease in fall temperatures was observed since mid-century.

Climate Divisions of Northwest Wyoming

The Twentieth Century increases in the 30-year precipitation averages that were observed at the scale of the GYE were not observed in the Divisional summaries (Drainages) (Figure 8); however, the increases in GYE annual temperatures were consistently observed in all three Drainages (Figure 9). The seasonal and temporal patterns of the summaries differ in magnitude and seasonality from the GYE summary, reflecting topography within the Drainages as well as their relationship to the summer-wet and winter-wet regimes. Elevations of the 19 stations used to describe the climate of the GYE ranged from 4744 to 7866 ft (1447 to 2400 m), and averaged 5960 ft (1818 m); thus, the data may reflect limitations of climate stations at higher elevations and probably represent climate from lower GYE elevations. GYE elevations span approximately 4000 to 14,000 ft (1220 to 4270 m).

In contrast to the patterns seen at the scale of the GYE, the 30-year annual precipitation averages declined throughout the Twentieth Century for the Yellowstone River and Wind River Drainages (see Figure 8). The Yellowstone and Wind River monthly precipitation patterns were more similar to

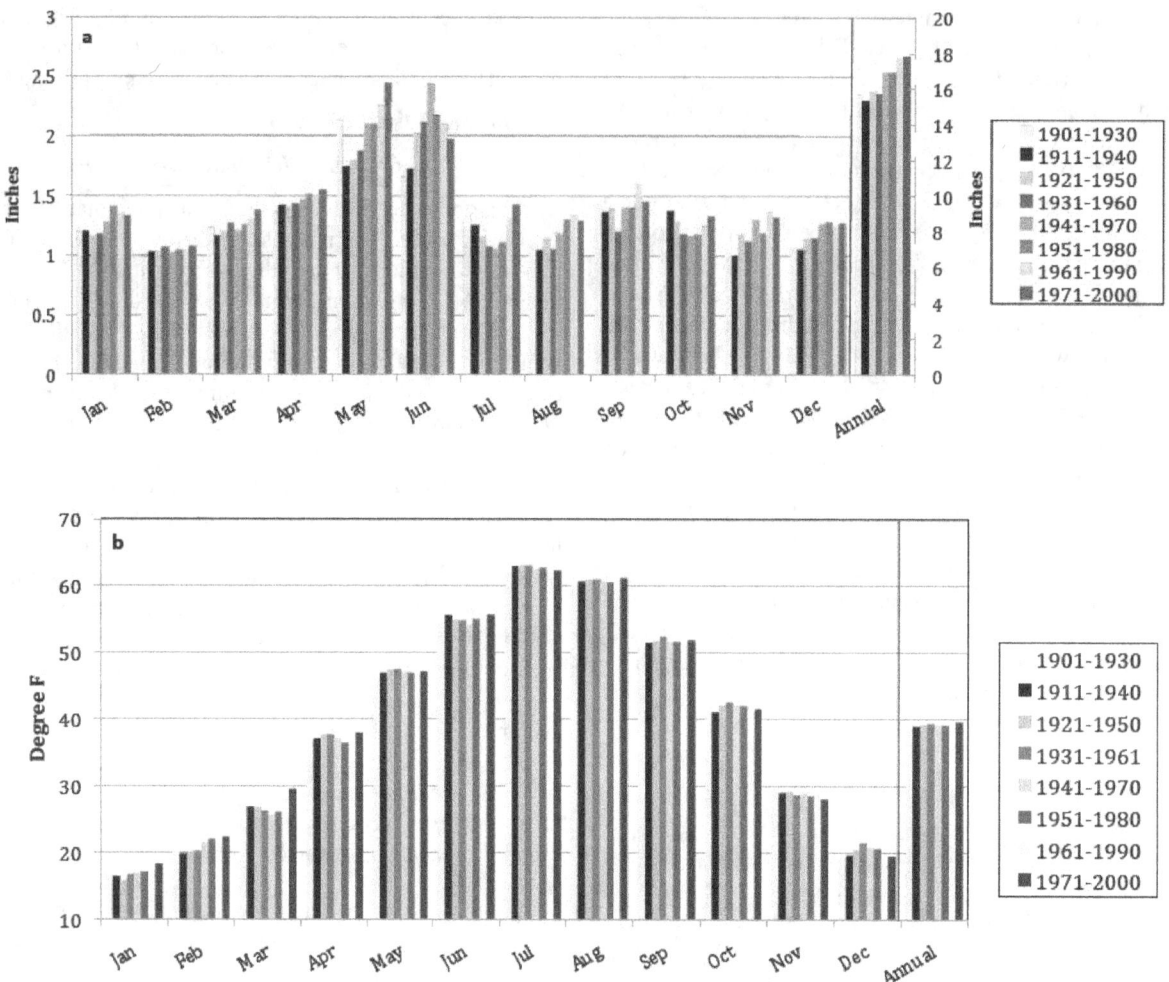

Figure 7. Mean monthly and annual precipitation (inches) and temperatures (°F) of the GYE Historic Climate Network stations. (a) 30-year means (annual precipitation on right axis, monthly precipitation on left axis) and (b) 30-year means for monthly and annual temperature.

each other than the Big Horn patterns. For Yellowstone River and Wind River Drainages, the 30-year precipitation averages for most months tended to drop throughout the Twentieth Century, whereas the Big Horn monthly values exhibited much variability over time. The Yellowstone River Drainage had its largest monthly decreases of precipitation during winter and in May, the Big Horn River Drainage had its largest monthly decreases during late summer and in May, and the Wind River Drainage had its largest monthly decreases during early fall and late spring (Figure 8). The Big Horn River and Wind River Drainages generally fall on the east side of the GYE, which are influenced more by a summer-wet precipitation regime in contrast to the western parts of the GYE (Figure 6).

In addition to reflecting the increases in 30-year average temperatures observed at the scale of the GYE, all three Drainages also showed the decline in fall temperatures observed at the GYE since mid-century (Figure 9). Annual temperatures for each 30-year period have increased 1 to 2 °F (0.6 to 1.1 °C) over the Twentieth Century, a much larger variation than at the GYE (Figure 7b). This difference may reflect the topographic variation within each division. The Yellowstone River Drainage encompasses northern portions of the Shoshone and YNP with few lower valley climate stations. While the Big Horn River and Wind River Drainages include climate stations from a larger number of lower valleys and towns, these Drainages also include the south and central Shoshone (Figure 2b). Monthly temperature averages have generally increased the most during winter (2 to 4 °F [1.1 to 2.2 °C]) at all Drainages, exceeding the variation in the GYE (Figure 9). Monthly temperature averages have decreased the most during fall (1 to 3 °F [0.6 to 1.7 °C]) at all Drainages. The Yellowstone River Drainage had the highest winter and summer temperature increases compared to the Big Horn River and Wind River Drainage. The variations in mean monthly temperature were greatest in the winter months and least in the summer months (Figure 9).

USDA Forest Service RMRS-GTR-264. 2012.

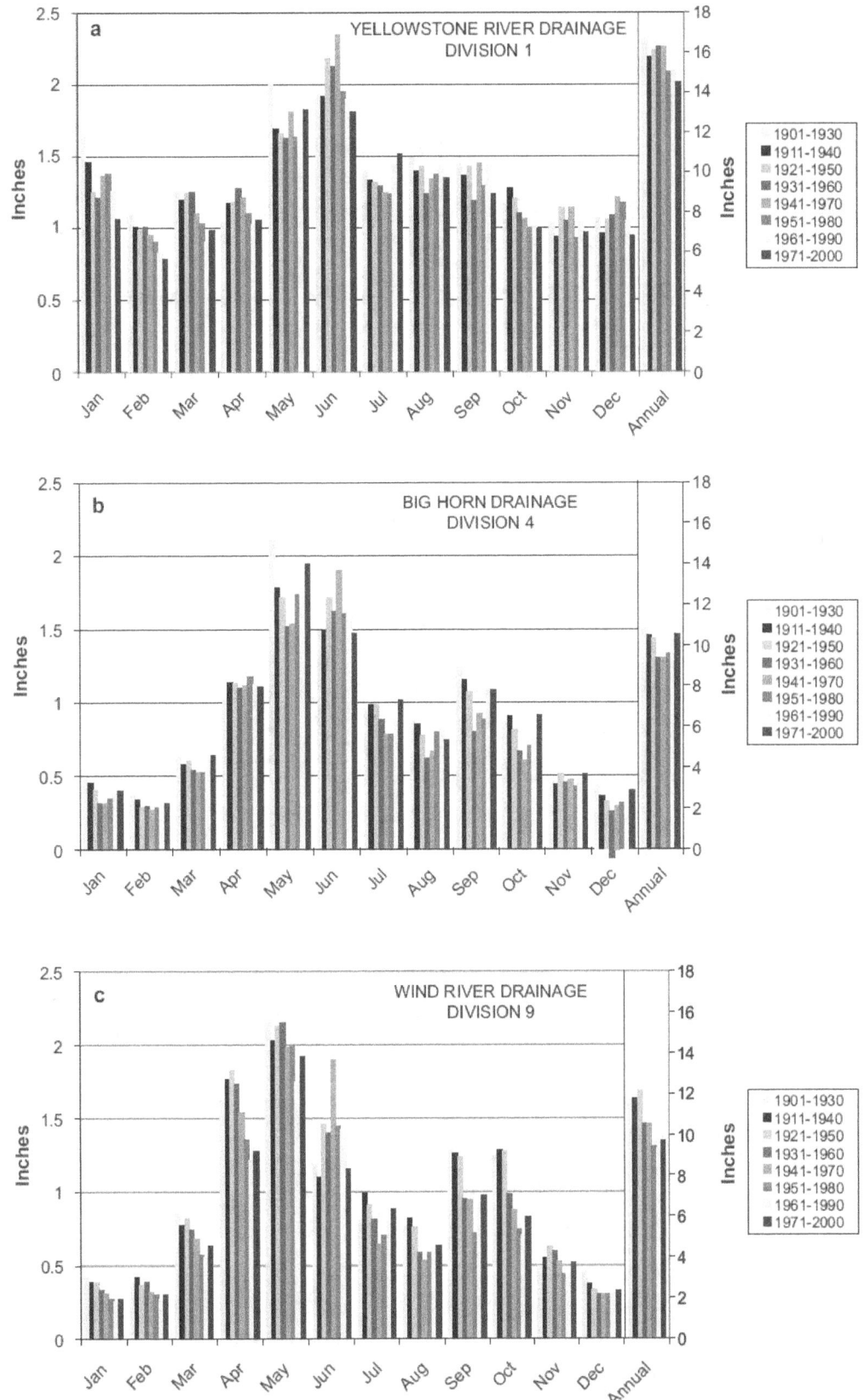

Figure 8. Mean monthly and annual precipitation 30-year averages (a, b, and c) (annual precipitation on right axis, monthly precipitation on left axis) for Climate Divisions 1, 4, and 9.

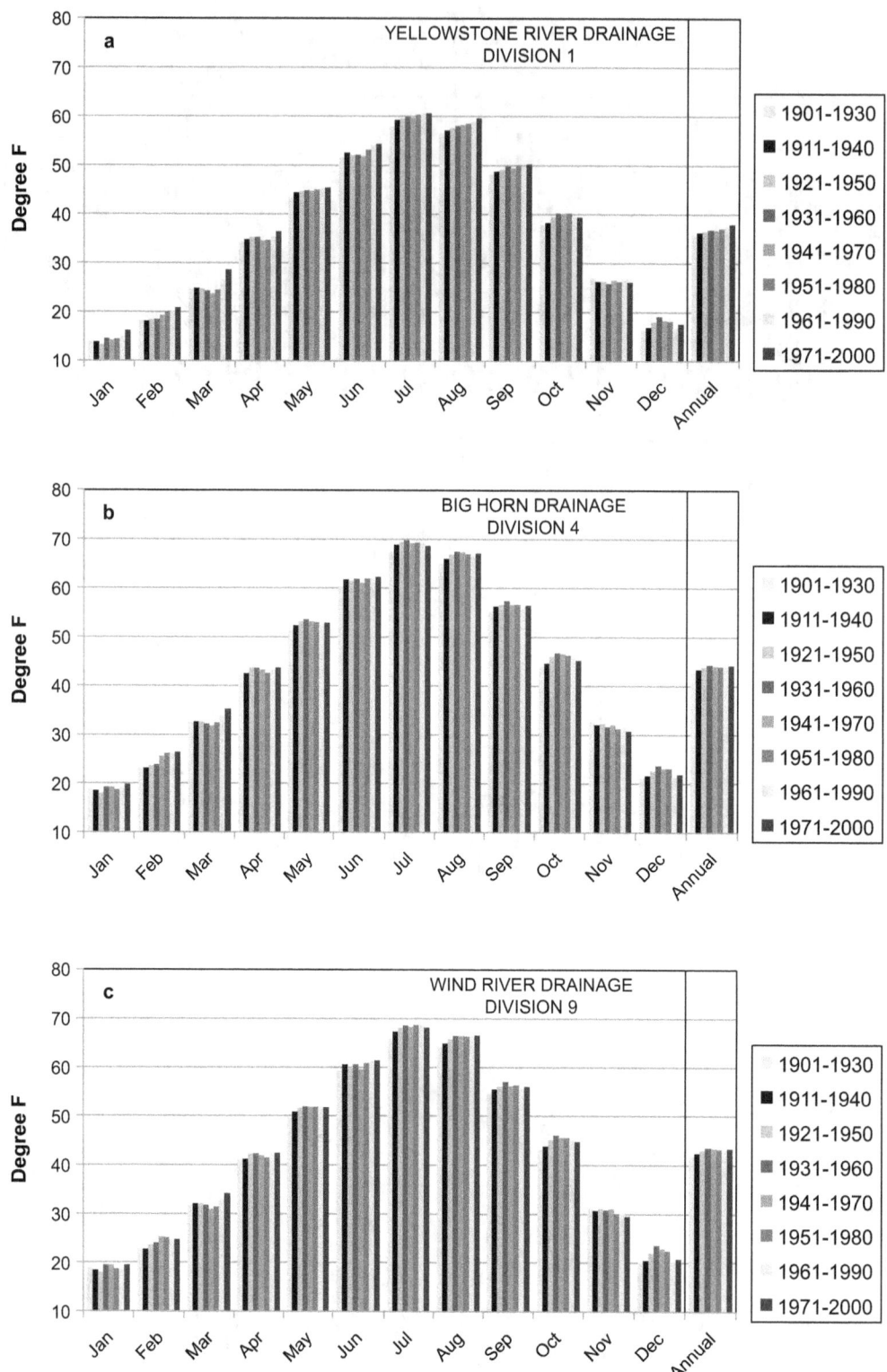

Figure 9. Monthly and annual temperature 30-year averages (a, b, and c) for Climate Divisions 1, 4, and 9.

The Shoshone Climate and SNOTEL Stations

The small set of stations within or near the Shoshone show averages for monthly and annual temperature and precipitation that range above and below the GYE averages (Figures 10 and 11). The three mountain ranges—Beartooth, Absaroka, and Wind River—provide orographic (the effect associated with mountains) variation along the 180 miles (290 km) north to south of the Shoshone (Figure 1). This topography creates a general east-west precipitation gradient in conjunction with the regional weather patterns—more precipitation occurs at higher elevations and less occurs at lower elevations and on the lee side of mountain ranges, which is generally the case with these six stations (Figure 10).

Higher-elevation areas in the western Shoshone experience wetter winters (Figure 6) because they receive winter storms from the Pacific air mass that moves in from the west. Summers are drier because these higher-elevation areas do not receive as much precipitation or intercept summer monsoonal flow from the south and east (Hansen 2006). The station with the highest precipitation is also the station with the shortest record—Yellowstone NP East Entrance. This station exhibits a more winter-wet precipitation regime, receiving highest monthly precipitation during December. Situated at 6952 ft (2119 m) on the boundary between YNP and the Shoshone, this station had a mean annual precipitation of 23 inches (584 mm) from 2000 to 2009 (Figure 10). The stations that exhibit more summer-wet conditions, receiving highest monthly precipitation during May and June are: Darwin Ranch, at the highest elevation (8160 ft [2489 m]) with 16 inches (406 mm) (36-year record); Crandall Creek (6640 ft [2025 m]) with 16 inches (406 mm)

(60-year record); South Pass at the second highest elevation (7840 ft [2391 m]) with 13 inches (330 mm) (110-year record); Buffalo Bill Dam (5160 ft [1574 m]) with 11 inches (279 mm) (104-year record); and Dubois (6955 ft [2121 m]) with 9 inches (229 mm) (104-year record) (Figure 11).

Darwin Ranch, at the highest elevation (8160 ft [2489 m]), has the lowest mean annual temperature of 31 °F (-0.6 °C) (1974 to 2009) (Figure 10). Located along the Gros Ventre River in a nearly flat 0.5 mile (0.8 km) wide valley with mountains on all sides rising 2000 to 3000 ft (610 to 915 m), the record low temperature at Darwin Ranch is -62 °F (-52 °C) (recorded February 10, 1981). South Pass, slightly lower in elevation (7840 ft [2391 m]), has a slightly higher mean annual temperature of 35 °F (1.7 °C) and a much longer weather record (1900 to 2009) (Figure 11). Buffalo Bill Dam, at the lowest elevation (5390 ft [1643 m]) and east of the Shoshone along the Shoshone River, has the warmest mean annual temperature of 47 °F (8.3 °C) (1905 to 2009). Dubois, also at lower elevation (6962 ft [2122 m]) and at the east boundary of the central Shoshone and northeast boundary of the Wind River Mountain Range, has the second warmest mean annual temperature of 40 °F (4.4 °C) (1905 to 2009) (Figures 10 and 11).

Crandall Creek is at 6600 ft (2013 m) in the northern part of the Shoshone with annual mean precipitation of 16 inches (406 mm), and a mean temperature of 38 °F (3.3 °C) (1948 to 2008). Located in Division 1, Crandall Creek shows a similar seasonal pattern to the Divisional data, with the greatest amount of precipitation coming in January, May, and June, and monthly temperatures the highest at around 60 °F (15.6 °C) in June. Monthly temperatures are the

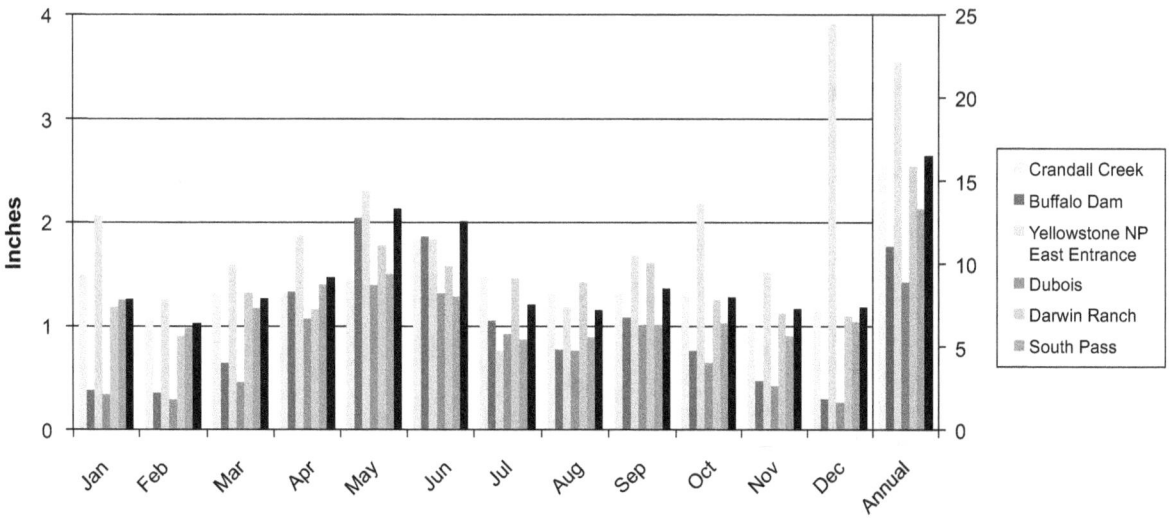

Figure 10. Mean monthly and annual precipitation (inches) for the period of record is shown for Crandall Creek (1948-2008), Buffalo Dam (1905-2009), Yellowstone National Park East Entrance (2000-2009), Dubois (1905-2009), Darwin Ranch (1974-2009), South Pass (1900-2009), and GYE Historical Climate Network station average (1901-2000) (from Western Regional Climate Center 2010; Historical Climate Network 2010) (annual precipitation is on right axis, monthly precipitation is on left axis).

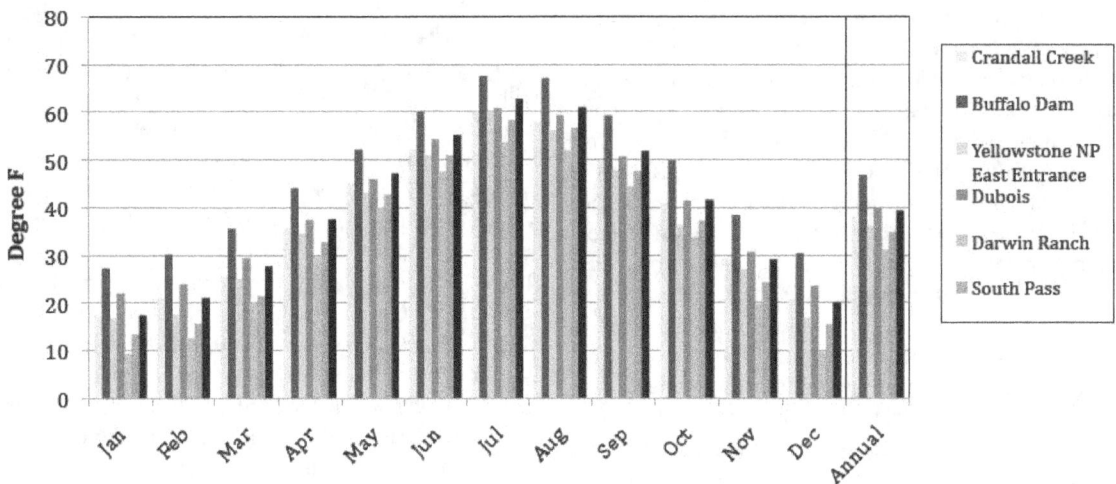

COOP Stations Average Monthly Temperature

Figure 11. Mean monthly and annual temperature (°F) for the period of record are shown for Crandall Creek (1948-2008), Buffalo Dam (1905-2009), Yellowstone National Park East Entrance (2000-2009), Dubois (1905-2009), Darwin Ranch (1974-2009), South Pass (1900-2009), and GYE Historical Climate Network station average (1901-2000) (from Western Regional Climate Center 2010; Historical Climate Network 2010).

highest at around 60 °F (15.6 °C) in July. However, January temperatures at Crandall Creek are warmer than the Division 1 average (Figures 10 and 11).

Yellowstone NP East Entrance has a mean annual temperature of 36 °F (2.2 °C) (2000 to 2009). This station and the Buffalo Bill Dam station are located in Division 4, and the average temperatures of these two stations bracket the annual temperature of the Division (Figure 9). Precipitation at Buffalo Bill Dam is close to the Division average whereas Yellowstone NP East Entrance precipitation is nearly twice the Division average. These station/Division differences reflect variation that can occur within a climate Division in western Wyoming and in the GYE (Figures 10 and 11).

Twenty SNOTEL sites, mostly within the Shoshone (Figure 2a and Appendix Table 3), span elevations from 7120 ft (2170 m) to 10,100 ft (3078 m), averaging 8986 ft (2739 m). Over the 30-year record, annual average temperature data of the combined SNOTEL sites (http://www.wcc. nrcs.usda.gov/snotel/Wyoming/wyoming html) show a statistically significant increasing trend (p<0.01) for minimum and maximum temperature (minimum temperature +2.6 °F/ decade [+1.4 °C/decade], and maximum temperature +1.3 °F /decade [+0.7 °C/decade]) (Figures 12 and 13). No statistically significant trend was found for snow water equivalent or precipitation. April average snow water equivalent averaged 2.7 inches (68.6 mm) and ranged from 0.6 to 7.9 inches (15.2 to 200.6 mm) (data not shown).

Figure 12. Shoshone SNOTEL sites annual average maximum temperature 1986-2009.

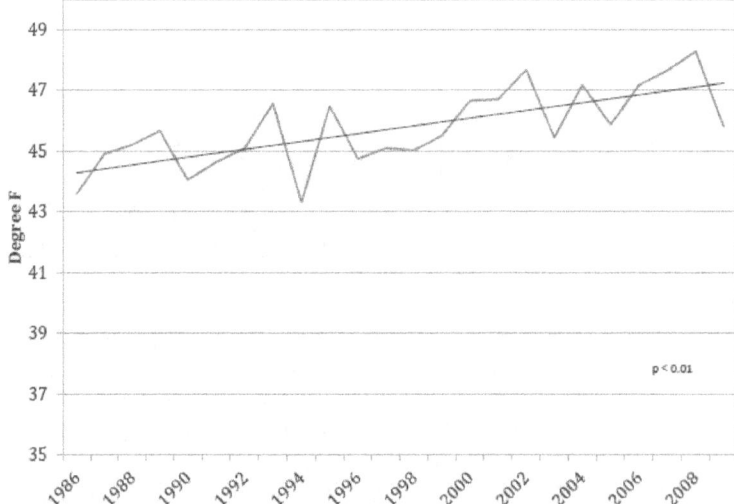

Annual Average Max Temperature

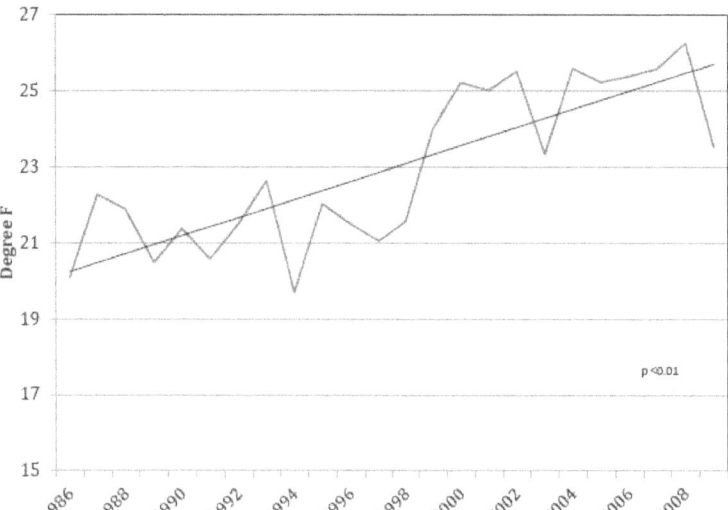

Figure 13. Shoshone SNOTEL sites annual average minimum temperature 1986-2009.

Over the Twentieth Century, several studies in the GYE have shown increases in annual temperature (Naftz and others 2002; Wilmers and Getz 2005; Hansen 2006; McWethy and others 2010), similar to patterns reported here (Figures 7b and 9). The GYE climate station average annual temperature for 1971 to 2000 is approximately 1 °F (0.6 °C) higher than the 1901 to 1930 annual average, reflecting similar increases seen in the Twentieth Century global mean temperature (IPCC 2007b). Using isotopic oxygen to reconstruct air temperatures from ice cores, Naftz and others (2002) found a 6.3 °F (3.5 °C) temperature increase from 1960 to the 1990s at 13,120 ft (4000 m) in the Wind River Range. The reconstructed air temperatures are comparable to other alpine sites around the world (Naftz and others 2002), however the recent rapid air temperature increase at this site in the Winter River Range may also reflect a shift in the proportion of snowfall from southerly storm tracks and moisture sources.

Wilmers and Getz (2005) found that the length of winter (defined by the number of days with snow on the ground) in the GYE has decreased since 1955. This decline is a function of both minimum and maximum temperatures increasing as well as days above 32 °F (0 °C) that caused a decline in snow depth since 1955 (Wilmers and Getz 2005). Increasing temperatures have led to earlier and longer growing seasons globally (Steltzer and Post 2009); growing seasons may have increased 15 to 20 days since 1970 (Penuelas and others 2009). Earlier and longer growing seasons have been noted in YNP (NPS 2009).

Greater Yellowstone Ecosystem Twentieth Century Precipitation Variability

Annual precipitation variability and drought conditions have intermittently existed over the last century in the GYE area (Gray and others 2007). Precipitation has varied on multi-decadal scales, with the worst drought periods occurring during the 1930s, 1950s, and 2000s (Balling and others 1992; Curtis and Grimes 2004; Hansen 2006; Gray and others 2007). GYE tree ring reconstructions of precipitation by Gray and others (2007) found the wettest year of the Twentieth Century was 1916 (20.3 inches/year or 516 mm/year precipitation) and the driest year was 1977 (11.6 inches/year or 295 mm/year precipitation). These reconstructions are representative of the east and north GYE with elevations that span 6800 and 8500 ft (2100 to 2600 m) (two locations in the central Shoshone Absaroka Mountains, and two sites north of YNP) (Figure 2). These precipitation extremes were likely equaled or exceeded at least 30 times in the past 600 years (Gray and others 2007).

Twentieth Century annual- and decadal-scale variability of GYE climate has been attributed to varied responses of El Niño Southern Oscillation (ENSO) events (Figure 14) and the Pacific Decadal Oscillation (PDO) (Figure 15) (Graumlich and others 2003; Gray and others 2007). Anomalously warm (El Niño) and cool (La Niña) sea surface temperatures in equatorial Pacific (El Niño Southern Oscillation [ENSO]) and north Pacific (Pacific Decadal Oscillation [PDO]) define warm and cool phases that inversely influence northwest and southwest United States climate and ecology (Rasmussen and Wallace 1983; Mantua and others 1997; Cayan and others 1999). The PDO has been observed to switch between a cool and warm phase every 10 to 30 years, while the ENSO switches phases every 3 to 7 years (Dettinger and others 1998).

The GYE lies near the transition zone between the Southwest and Pacific Northwest response types to ENSO (Despain 1987; Whitlock and Bartlein 1993; Gray and others 2007). The Pacific Northwest and northern Rocky Mountains are generally drier than average during El Niño years and wetter than average during La Niña years (Hunter and others 2006; Gray and others 2007). The winter-wet regions of the GYE (Figure 6) exhibit Pacific Northwest responses (in other words, drier during El Niño), especially during the winter (Graumlich and others 2003). Conversely, the Southwest United States and summer-wet regions of the

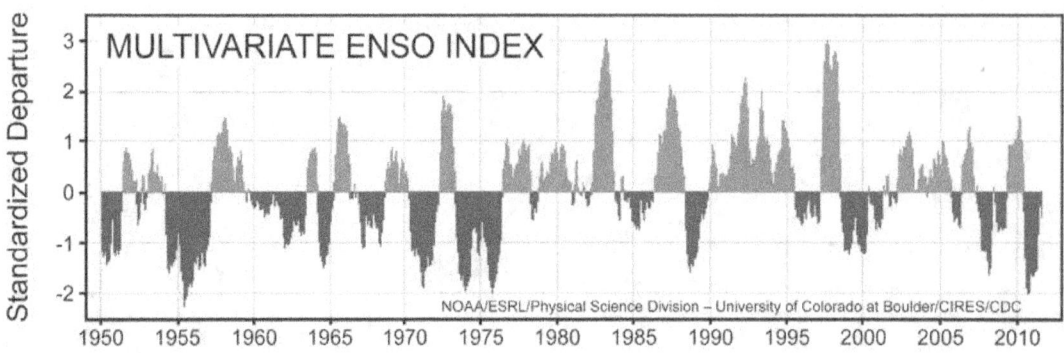

Figure 14. El Nino Southern Oscillation (ENSO) from 1950-2010. Source: NOAA http://www.esrl. noaa.gov/psd/people/klaus.wolter/MEI/.

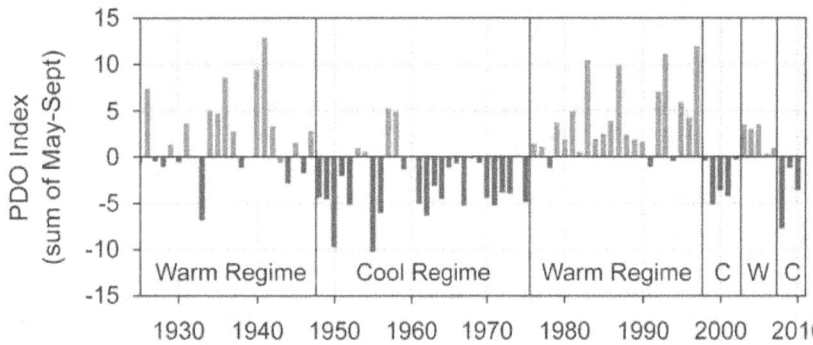

Figure 15. Pacific Decadal Oscillation (PDO) from 1950-2010. Source: NOAA http://www.nwfsc.noaa.gov/ research/divisions/fed/oeip/ ca-pdo.cfm.

GYE (Figure 6) typically demonstrate the opposite response (wetter during El Niño). The GYE may also show no significant response to ENSO at all, thus, the mean response of the GYE to an ENSO event likely depends upon the magnitude of sea surface temperature anomalies (Gray and others 2007). However, there is some uncertainty regarding the overall strength of the ENSO effect in the GYE because of complications due to elevation effects and the relative dearth of meteorological data, especially from high-elevation sites (Hansen 2006).

Sea surface temperatures associated with the PDO also influence decadal variability in GYE precipitation (Graumlich and others 2003). In the northern Rocky Mountains, winters have more precipitation and are cooler during the cool PDO phase, while the warm phase is associated with drier winters (Mantua and others 1997). Graumlich and others (2003) found that winter precipitation in the south and central summer-dry region of the GYE closely follows the PDO on decadal time scales, while ENSO exerts more influence on annual time scales.

Historic Climate of the Shoshone National Forest and Greater Yellowstone Ecosystem: 20,000 BP to the Twentieth Century

Historic climate of the Shoshone is inferred from climatological studies that are focused largely in YNP with fewer sites in the GYE (Figure 3). The Shoshone average elevation (9100 ft or 2773 m) is over 1000 ft higher than YNP (Lueneburg 2007), and more than 25 percent of the Shoshone (625,000 acres or 252,930 ha) is above tree line (USDA Forest Service 2009c). The Shoshone is more topographically complex than YNP, which is situated on the flatter Yellowstone Plateau (see Figure 1). The historic climate described for the GYE may be more characteristic of areas west of the Shoshone and should be considered in the context of the observation's location and elevation. Although most descriptions of paleoclimates in the GYE focus on YNP, many of the long-term, large-scale trends (for example, temperature trends and shifting of jet stream) hold true for the Shoshone as well.

The climate of the GYE has varied over the last 20,000 years (Figure 16), and the most important control of climate in the GYE on large time scales (10^3 to 10^4 years) has been the tilt of the Earth's axis and the timing of perihelion (the point of orbit at which the earth is closest to the sun) (Kutzbach and Guetter 1986; Whitlock 1993; Millspaugh and others 2000). During the last glacial maximum 20,000 BP, temperatures in the region were ~5 to ~20 °F (~2.8 to ~11.1 °C) colder than present with less precipitation (Brocoli and Manabe 1987; Whitlock 1993). The entire northern hemisphere warmed from 20,000 to 10,000 BP as the tilt of the Earth increased. Temperatures increased slightly by 18,000 to 15,000 BP (approximately 13 °F [7.2 °C] cooler than present at mid-latitudes) due to the southern branch of the jet stream being shifted south by the continental ice sheet (Whitlock 1993). By 14,000 to 12,000 BP, temperatures increased to 4 to 9 °F (2 to 5 °C) cooler than present and the ice sheet was reduced to 50 percent of its full-glacial height (Whitlock 1993). Temperatures were only 1 to 4 °F (0.6 to 2.2 °C) cooler than present at Yellowstone Lake by 11,550 ± 350 BP (Baker 1970).

Approximately 10,000 BP, perihelion occurred in the summer, as opposed to today's winter occurrence, creating the greatest contrast in winter and summer insolation (a measure of solar radiation) in the past 20,000 years (Kutzbach and Guetter 1986; Whitlock 1993; Millspaugh and others 2000). Around 10,000 BP, insolation at GYE latitudes was 8.5 percent greater than present in the summer, and 10 percent less than present in the winter (Berger 1978; Millspaugh and others 2000). Summer temperatures were 1 to 4 °F (0.6 to 2.2 °C) warmer than present as a direct result of greater summer insolation, and moisture decreased (Fall and others 1995; Bartlein and others 1998; Huerta and others 2009). Concurrently, seasonal amplification of solar radiation indirectly enhanced summer drought in the region by causing an expansion of the Pacific subtropical high-pressure system (Whitlock 1993; Whitlock and Bartlein 1993). Climate simulations also suggest moist air flowed into the GYE during the early Holocene (11,000 to 8000 BP) because of intensified monsoonal circulation, also a result of seasonal solar radiation amplification (Whitlock 1993; Bartlein and others 1998; Millspaugh and others 2000; Huerta and others 2009). Thus, the northern GYE was likely wetter than present between 11,000 and 8000 BP (Figure 16).

Around 9500 BP, the climate of the GYE split between two distinct regions: north (summer-wet/winter-dry) and south (summer-dry/winter-wet) (Whitlock 1993; Whitlock and Bartlein 1993; Huerta and others 2009) (see Figure 6). Based on vegetation reconstructions of pollen records from lake sediment (locations in Figure 3), Whitlock and Bartlein (1993) and Huerta and others (2009) suggested the GYE northern (summer-wet/winter-dry) region exhibited wetter-than-present conditions between 9500 to 7000 BP and then became steadily more arid until 3000 BP, while the southern (summer-dry/winter-wet) region was drier at about 9000 BP and steadily became wetter until 3000 BP. Pollen records from ~9840 ft (~3001 m) in the Wind River Range showed that maximum warmth and aridity occurred around 5400 BP (Fall and others 1995). Cooler and moister conditions persisted in the region after 3000 BP until the Medieval Warm Period, about 1000 BP (Hansen 2006; Huerta and others 2009). However, there is some evidence from high-elevation sites in the Wind River Range that summer temperatures were still warmer than today around 3000 BP (Fall and others 1995) (Figure 16).

The GYE also warmed during the Medieval Warm Period (about 1000 BP) and, as a whole, experienced drought conditions (Gray and others 2007). The end of the Little Ice Age (1860 to 1890) marked the coldest and wettest conditions in the GYE in the previous 700 years (Gray and others 2007).

This was especially true at higher elevations, where ice core evidence from Fremont Glacier (13,120 ft [4002 m]) in the Wind River Range indicates that temperatures were approximately 9 °F (~5 °C) cooler than present during the Little Ice Age (Naftz and others 2002) (Figure 16). During the Twentieth Century, temperatures in the GYE have generally increased ~1 °F (~0.6 °C) and potentially from 4 to 6 °F (2.2 to 3.3 °C) at higher elevations (see the "Temporal Climate Patterns" section).

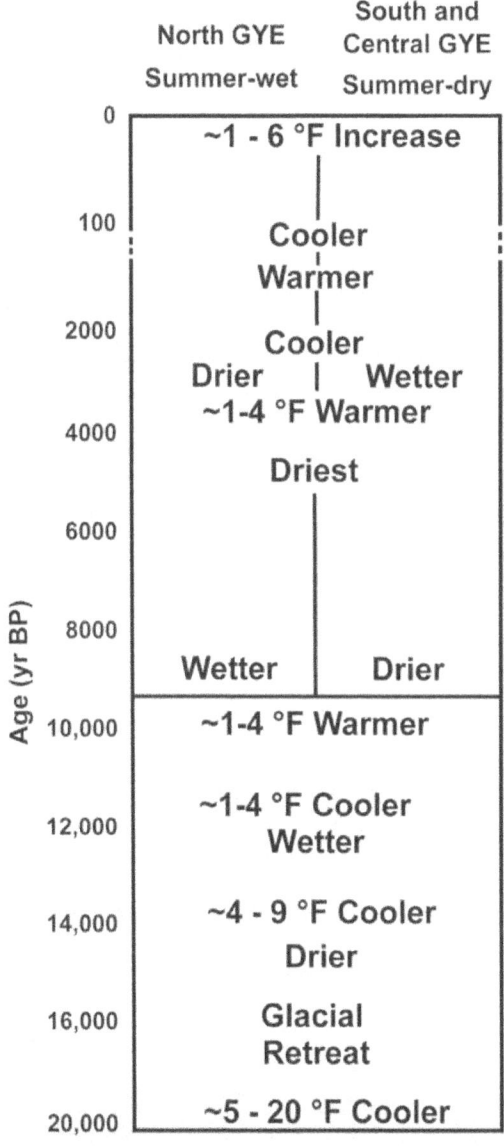

Figure 16. Historic climate of the GYE.

Future Climate on the Shoshone National Forest

Climate Projections

Atmospheric science is continually improving the understanding of and the ability to model the processes that influence global climate. Analysis of the results of climate models from research centers around the world is reported in the IPCC (2007a), and the output from these global climate models is archived by the Coupled Model Intercomparison Project, Phase 3 (Meehl and others 2007). Climate simulations are included in this large data set that scientists around the world can access. This additional analysis provides insight into the strengths and weaknesses of these models.

Projecting future climate involves not only understanding the dynamics of the global climate but also developing a story line for how the world economy and population growth might affect the emissions of greenhouse gases, which alter the chemistry of the climate. Three greenhouse gas emission scenarios were developed in the Special Report on Emissions Scenarios and are called A1B, A2, and B1 to avoid judging the effects of these scenarios. For each scenario, the world economies and population growth into the future varies. These scenarios offer a range of potential future global average surface warming: B1 is +3.2 °F (+1.8 °C), A1B is +5 °F (+2.8 °C), and A2 is +6.1 °F (+3.4 °C) for 2090 to 2100 relative to 1980 to 1999 (IPCC 2007b).

The global climate models simulate climate at a coarse spatial scale—large grid cells exceed 124 miles (200 km) on a side. To explore the finer scale of climate, these global projections are downscaled using a variety of techniques. For the Rapid-Response Climate Assessment for the Fish and Wildlife Service, Ray and others (2010) downscaled global projections for the western United States to a 2.4-mile (4-km) spatial scale using the delta method. Using the same information, McWethy and others (2010) summarized the projections for the Rocky Mountains and Upper Columbia Basin.

The global models show warming for large parts of the world, including North America (IPCC 2007b). Focusing on the results from an ensemble of 22 climate models used in the Fourth Assessment Report of the Intergovernmental Panel on Climate Change (IPCC 2007a), McWethy and others (2010) described changes by 2050 for the GYE as ranging from +3 °F (+1.7 °C) for annual temperature, to +4 °F (+2.2 °C) for winter temperature, to +5 °F (+2.8 °C) for summer temperatures, relative to the 1950 to 1999 period. Precipitation was described as increasing between 0 and 10 percent annually and in the winter, whereas summer precipitation was modeled to decline about 10 percent. However, McWethy and others (2010) noted that changes in the amount and spatial distribution of precipitation were still poorly understood and difficult to project.

Statistically downscaled projections of summer temperatures show a shift in temperature zones northward and upward in elevation across the western Pacific Northwest, including the GYE (McWethy and others 2010; Ray and others 2010).

Ray and others (2010) concluded that by 2050, the warming signal may be clearly seen throughout the western United States. To further explore the potential changes in temperature at locations that represent pika habitats, Ray and others (2010) downscaled climate projections to 22 specific grid cells that either were locations of known pika habitats or a local summit chosen as a representative. No locations in the Shoshone were included in Ray and others' (2010) analysis; however locations in the nearby National Forests of the Bighorn, Wind River/Bridger Teton, and Gallatin were represented (Table 1). At these three locations, the 2050 summer temperature projections are consistently higher than the 1950 to 1999 PRISM mean temperatures, and the projected temperature exceeds the 90th percentile of the 1950 to 1999 summer temperatures (Table 1). For example, the 1950 to 1999 average temperature for the Gallatin National Forest grid was 50.7 °F (10.4 °C), and the projected temperature for 2050 is 56.2 °F (13.44 °C). For the grids within these three National Forests, the lowest summer projection is higher than the 90th percent of the 1950 to 1999 period, suggesting that the coolest summers of the mid-Twenty-First Century will be warmer than the warmest summers of the last 50 years in the Twentieth Century (Table 1).

To interpret potential future climate change, we summarize observed Twentieth Century climate, and projections for the Twenty-First Century in Table 2. McWethy and others (2010) stressed that natural variations in climate and the accompanying ecological response occur at multiple temporal and spatial scales.

Studies across the western United States have described observed changes in climate: warmer annual temperature, winter warming more than summer, nighttime temperature warming more than daytime, increased intensity of rainfall events, more rain versus snow within the winter season, earlier peak runoff, and changes in fire regimes. While a number of studies have explored these data, climate stations within northwest Wyoming are not often included in these studies. For example, Knowles and others (2006: Figure 1a) documented the shift of winter snowfall to rainfall across the United States; however, no station data were available for northwest Wyoming. Similarly, data quality limitations eliminated nearly all northwest Wyoming climate stations in Kunkel and others' (2003) analysis of temporal variations of extreme precipitation events. Further, assessing climate patterns within the GYE is complicated because of the topographic variability as well as the location of the GYE in a transition area between northwestern and southwestern circulation patterns. McWethy and others (2010) noted that variations in the climate dynamics that influence these circulations patterns often result in opposite trends in climatic conditions at sites within the same region (see also Gray and others 2007).

Projections for future climatic conditions in the GYE include increasing temperatures annually and potentially increased but highly variable precipitation. The projected increase in temperatures suggests that more extreme temperature episodes will occur; the coolest of the future summer projections was warmer than most summers in the historical period.

Table 1. Mid-Century average temperature projections and extremes compared with historical climate data for summer seasons at single locations within three Na ional Forests in Wyoming. This analysis was developed as part of the Rapid-Response Climate Assessment for the Fish and Wildlife Service on pika (Ray and others 2010). Historical climate informa ion is based on PRISM. Summer season is June-July-August (JJA).

Single location within each National Forest (NF)	Gridbox latitude, longitude	Mean gridbox elevation ft (m)	Pika site elevation (ft)	JJA 10th percentile (1950-1999) °F (°C)	JJA Mean (1950-1999) °F (°C)	JJA 90th percentile (1950-1999) °F (°C)	Low model (10th percentile A1B [2040-2060] °F (°C)	JJA CMIP projection mean (2040-2060) °F (°C)	High model (90th percentile A1B [2040-2060] °F (°C)
Gallatin NF	45.44, -110.94	9167.4 (2778)	9180	48.7 (9.27)	50.7 (10.39)	52.5 (11.38)	54.1 (12.25)	56.2 (13.44)	58.7 (14.84)
Wind River/Bridger-Teton	43.19, -109.69	12153.9 (3683)	*	40.7 (4.81)	43.3 (6.3)	46.3 (7.97)	47.1 (8 39)	49.2 (9.55)	51.7 (10.96)
Bighorn NF	44.44, -107.19	12048 3 (3651)	*	43.3 (6.25)	44.9 (7.19)	46.5 (8.04)	48.2 (8 99)	50.3 (10.17)	52.6 (11.44)

*No information

Table 2. Observed 20th Century and future climate projections of temperature and precipitation for the GYE and Shoshone.

	Observed 20th Century	Climate projections
GYE	• Annual temperature increases range from 2 to 4 °F (1 to 2 °C) with greatest increases in the second half of the 20th Century • Temperature increases more pronounced in winter and spring • April soil water equivalent from snow courses over 1960 to 2002 show declines in most basins in northwest Wyoming • Precipitation highly variable, with the 1930s and 1950s significantly drier than average, although prolonged droughts in the last millennia rival these 20th Century droughts in duration and magnitude	• Annual temperature increases projected to be 3 °F (1.7 °C) by 2050 • Ranges for increases in annual temperature by 2100 are from 2 to 10 °F (1.1 to 5.5 °C) • Winter temperatures are projected to increase 4 °F (2.2 °C) relative to 1950 to 1999 • Summer temperatures are projected to increase 5 °F (2.7 °C) relative to 1950 to 1999 • Annual precipitation is projected to increase by 10 percent. Winter precipitation increases of 10 percent and summer precipitation decreases of 10 percent. (Precipitation projections are more uncertain as about half of the Global Circulation Model projections agree.)
Shoshone	• Topography creates an east-west precipitation gradient with more precipitation occurring at western higher elevations and less at eastern lower elevations • Western higher elevations experience wetter winters—the result of winter storms from the Pacific air masses—and have summer-dry climate. Eastern and lower elevations lie in a rain shadow where moisture from Pacific flow is intercepted by mountains to the west. However, these areas have a summer-wet climate, receiving summer monsoonal flow.	• Annual temperature increases projected to be 3 °F (1.7 °C) by 2050 • Ranges for increases in annual temperature by 2100 are from 2 to 10 °F (1.1 to 5.5 °C) • Winter temperatures are projected to increase 4 °F (2.2 °C) relative to 1950 to 1999 • Summer temperatures are projected to increase 5 °F (2.7 °C) relative to 1950 to 1999 • Annual precipitation is projected to increase by 10 percent. Winter precipitation increases of 10 percent and summer precipitation decreases of 10 percent. (Precipitation projections are more uncertain as about half of the Global Circulation Model projections agree.)

Climate Projections Used in Existing Ecological Response Models

Eighteen modeling studies associated with the Shoshone and outlying areas use climate projections to analyze the effects on ecosystems for scales that range from global and western hemisphere, to the western or entire United States, to the GYE and YNP regions (Table 3). Given that the first study was published in 1991, vintage of climate model and projection differs across these studies. The ability of climate models to quantify processes that include global climate, such as atmosphere interaction with oceans, has improved over the last 20 years. In this section, we describe these climate projections that have been used in ecological response models in light of recent studies exploring the future impact of climate in the Shoshone and GYE region.

Types of climate models are: Atmosphere-Ocean Global Circulation Models (AOGCMs), Global Circulation Models (GCMs), and Regional Circulation Models (RegCM). The ecological models that quantify the ecosystem response include Dynamic Global Vegetation Models (DGVMs), Bioclimate Envelope Models, Equilibrium Vegetation Models, and a variety of regression and qualitative techniques. These climate models and projections have also been useful in assessing the historical relationships between past climate and fire regimes, glacier changes, or lake dynamics as well as future effects of climate change (Table 3). The temperature and precipitation projections used in these response models vary over time as some studies use earlier versions of climate models. One study by Romme and Turner (1991) used qualitative methods to infer ecosystem responses under a warmer-wetter and warmer-drier situation.

Interpretation of the results of these studies for management use must consider what climate future was explored, how that climate future compares to other studies exploring the same natural resource, and how that climate future compares to what is now thought to be the future climate for the Shoshone and the GYE. For example, Bartlein and others (1997) incorporated a very wet future—100 percent change in winter precipitation—into their analysis and described the modern climate analogue to this projection as occurring in northwestern Montana and northern Idaho. In contrast, Diffenbaugh and others (2003) assumed no change to a decline in annual precipitation in their study. Comparing temperature projections across studies, Bachelet and others (2001) used temperature projections that span a range of 7 °F (4 °C) in contrast to the 2.7 °F (1.5 °C) range used by Shafer and others (2001). Many of these studies used projections that describe a future with increased precipitation; McWethy and others (2010) characterized the increases in future precipitation as less certain.

Future Temperature

The modeling studies in Table 3 used several scenarios that project temperatures that range from 2 to 18 °F (1 to 10 °C) to capture a range of potential future temperature conditions. The GCM projections used as input for environmental response models by Bartlein and others (1997) and Smithwick and others (2009) had the highest temperature increases and assumed a doubling of CO_2 (Table 3). Bartlein and others (1997) used GCM-projected temperature increases of approximately 9 to 18 °F (5 to 10 °C), and Smithwick and others (2009) used a temperature increase that ranged from 5 to 16.4 °F (2.8 to 9.1 °C). The other modeling studies in Table 3 utilized more modest temperature increases that ranged from 2 to 12 °F (1 to 6.7 °C). The most extensive projections were from Christensen and others (2007) who used a multi-model ensemble of 21 GCMs and Lawler and others (2009) who used an ensemble of 10 AOGCMs. Both used several scenarios of temperature increases ranging from 2 to 10 °F (1.1 to 5.5 °C). Study resolutions spanned from 0.6 to 37 miles (1 km to 60 km).

Future Precipitation

Projections of precipitation are more variable and uncertain than temperature projections (IPCC 2007b). The A1B simulations used by Christensen and others (2007) include an ensemble of several AOGCMs and project a modest increase in precipitation during winter (~10 percent more annual precipitation) for most of North America, including the Shoshone (Table 3). Yellowstone regionally based (regional and downscaled GCM) projections for annual precipitation range from no increase to a 50 percent increase (Table 3). Winter precipitation is projected to increase, and summer precipitation has a projected small decrease to no change (Bartlein and others 1997; Diffenbaugh and others 2003; Hall and Farge 2003; Whitlock and others 2003; Schrag and others 2008; Smithwick and others 2008). Bartlein and others (1997) indicated winter precipitation may increase on the Shoshone but not as much as projected for YNP (Bartlein and others 1997: Figure 2). Most of the climate projections used as input for response models in Table 3 project an increase in winter precipitation, while summer precipitation is expected to remain the same or decrease. Understanding how the precipitation projections and corresponding temperature projections interact is important; McWethy and others (2010) suggested that increased precipitation is unlikely to offset increased evapotranspiration associated with even a modest warming of 0.6 to 1.1 °F (1 to 2 °C).

Future Temperature and Precipitation Changes Used in Ecological Impact Models

The projected range of annual temperature changes for the GYE is 2 to 10 °F (1.1 to 18 °C), and the projected range of precipitation change is no change to a 10 percent increase (McWethy and others 2010). When these ranges are compared to the range of future changes used in the current impacts literature, one can see that many of the impact models explored a greater range of possible futures (Figure 17). These differences reflect the nature of the scenarios (IPCC or a simple twice the ambient carbon dioxide [CO_2]concentration) and which climate models were used. While these studies offer much information, the results must be compared in light of climate projections since the climate ranges differ greatly among these studies.

Table 3. Climate scenarios and projections used in modeling studies exploring the ecological responses to climate change effects on the GYE or larger geographic areas.

Study (region)	GCM model	Response models	Resolution	Future scenario	Ending CO$_2$ (ppm)	Temperature change °F (°C)	Precipitation change (%)	By year
Bachelet and others (2001) (U.S.)	HADCM2GH, HADCM2SU, CGCM1, UKMO, GISS, GFDL-R30, OSU	MAPPS, MC1 (Vegetation)	10 km	IPCC First Assessment Report, 2 x CO$_2$	712	+4 to +12 (+2.2 to +6.6)	+2 to +30	2099
Bachelet and others (2003) (U.S.)	HADCM2SUL, CGCM1	MC1, LPJ (Vegetation)	10 km	IPCC First Assessment Report, 2 x CO$_2$	712	+4 to +10 (+2.2 to +5.5)	+23	2100
Bartlein and others (1997) (GYE)	CCC	Equilibrium (Vegetation)	25 km	2 x CO$_2$	724	+9 to +18 (+5 to +10)	+100 in winter, almost no summer change	2100
Bradley and others (2009) (West U.S.)	10 AOGCMs	Bioclimate Envelope Model (Invasive Vegetation)	4.5 km	IPCC Fourth Assessment Report, A1B	700	+3 to +8 (+1.7 to +4.4)	-47 to +72	2100
Christensen and others (2007) (Global)	Multi-model ensemble of several types of climate models (PCMDI)		Global Various	IPCC Fourth Assessment Report, All Scenarios	500 to 1000	+2 to +10 (+1.1 to +5.5)	-20 to +20	2100
Diffenbaugh and others (2003) (West U.S.)	RegCM2.5, CCM3.6.6	BIOME4 (Vegetation)	40 km	2 x CO$_2$	560	+4 to +11 (+2.2 to +6)	0 to -10	*
Gray and McCabe (2010)	Multi-model average	Water Balance Model	*	IPCC Fourth Assessment Report, A1B Average	715	+1.5 (+0.88) +3 (+1.7) +6.1 (+3.4)	Based on historic tree ring records	2025,205 0,2100
Hall and Fagre (2003) (Glacier National Park)	GISS, GFDL, OSU	GLACier Prediction	*	IPCC First Assessment Report, 2 x CO$_2$	704	+5.4 (+3.3)	+5 to +10	2100
Hostetler and Giorgi (1995) (Pyramid and Yellowstone Lakes)	MM4 RegCM nested in GENESIS GCM	Lake Model	60 km	2 x CO$_2$	718	+5.5 to +6 (+3 to +3.4)	+17 to +22	2100

Table 3. *Continued.*

Study (region)	GCM model	Response models	Resolution	Future scenario	Ending CO$_2$ (ppm)	Temperature change °F (°C)	Precipitation change (%)	By year
Lawler and others (2009) (Western Hemisphere)	10 AOGCMs	Bioclimate Envelope (Vegetation)	50 km	IPCC Fourth Assessment Report B1, A1B, A2	500 to 1200	+2 to +10 (+1.1 to +5.5)	-20 to +20	2100
Rehfeldt and others (2009) (Western U.S.)	CGCM3, GFDLCM2.1, HADCM3	Climate Envelope (Vegetation)	1 km	IPCC Fourth Assessment Report B1, B2, A2	500 to 1200	+2 to +9 (+1 to +5)	-10 to +6	2100
Romme and Turner (1991) (GYE)	Qualitative	Qualitative	Qualitative	Warm-dry, Warm-wet	*	*	*	*
Schlaepfer and others (2011)	Composite of 16	Sagebrush Bioclimate	10 km	IPCC Fourth Assessment Report B1 and A2	500-1200	+2 to +9 (+1 to +5)	*	2100
Schrag and others (2008) (Yellowstone and Grand Teton National Parks)	Based on Bartlein and others (1997)	Random Forest (Tree-line prediction)	*	Based on Bartlein and others (1997)	*	0 and +8 (0 and +4.5)	0 and +35	*
Shafer and others (2001) (North America)	HADCM2, CGCM1, and CSIRO	Regression of bioclimate variables (vegetation)	25 km	Annual 1% compound increase in GHG (IPCC IS92a)	700	+2.7 (+1.5)	Not available	2100
Smithwick and others (2009) (Yellowstone National Park)	HADCM2	CENTURY Climate Envelope (vegetation)	~55 km grid cell centered at Old Faithful	*	708	Min / Max +5 / +11 (+2.8 / +4.7)	+22	2100
	CCC 1				708	+7.7 / +16.4 (+4.3 / +9.1)	+12	2100
Stonefeldt and others (2000) Wind River, Wyoming	Nested RCM (NCAR/Penn State)	Soil Water Assessment Tool (SWAT)	*	2 x CO$_2$	660	+4 (+2.2)	-10 to +10	2100
Whitlock and others (2003) (GYE)	HADCM2 HCGSa	Regression	*	Annual 1% compound increase in CO$_2$	940	*	*	2059

*Information not available

Abbreviations: AOGCM = Atmospheric-Ocean Global Circulation Model; CO$_2$ = Carbon dioxide concentration; CCC, CCC1 = Canadian Climate Centre; CGCM1 = Canadian Global Coupled Model; CSIRO = Commonwealth Science and Industrial Research Organisation, Australia; GISS = Goddard Institute for Space Studies (NASA) model; GFDL, GFDL-R30 = Geophysical Fluid Dynamics Laboratory; GHG = greenhouse gases; HADCM, HADCM2GH, HADCM2SU, HADCM2 = Hadley Centre Climate Model; HCGSa = Hadley Centre Greenhouse Gas Sulfate Aerosol; LPJ = Lund, Potsdam, Jena Dynamic Global Vegetation Model; MAPPS = Mapped Atmosphere-Plant-Soil System Vegetation Model; MC1 = MAPPS – CENTURY Dynamic Global Vegetation Model; MM4 RegCM = Mesoscale model Regional Climate Model (NCAR); NCAR = National Center for Atmospheric Research, Boulder, Colorado; Nested RCM = Nested Regional Climate Model; OSU = Oregon State University model; PCMDI = Program for Climate Model Diagnosis and Intercomparison, Lawrence Livermore National Laboratory, California; UKMO = United Kingdom Meterological Office Model.

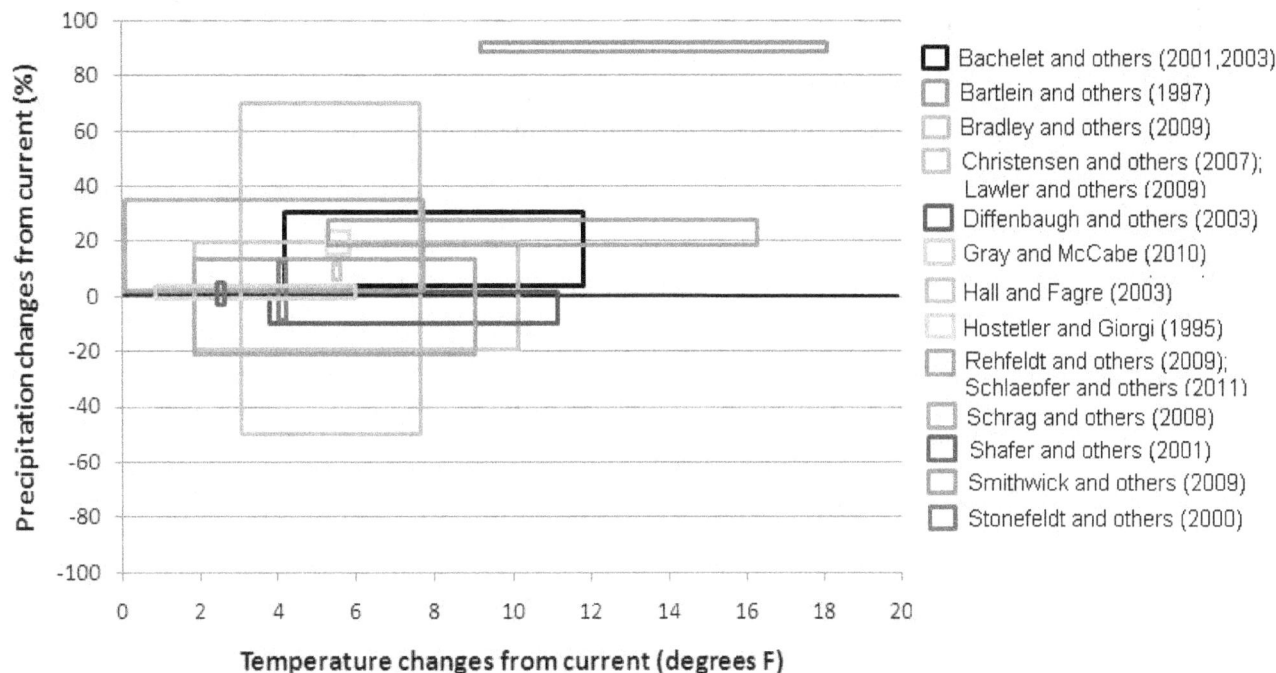

Figure 17. Future temperature and precipitation range changes used in ecological impact models.

Climate Change Effects on Ecosystems: Observed Trends and Future Projections

Introduction

At the national scale, U.S. temperatures have warmed about 1.5 °F (0.8 °C) over the last 100 years (Karl and others 2009); studies focused on the western United States and the GYE suggest that similar increases in temperature have been documented, with some effects also noted in the physical and ecological characteristics of the GYE and western United States ecosystems (Naftz and others 2002; Wilmers and Getz 2005; Hansen 2006; McWethy and others 2010). The projected changes in climate, particularly the increasing temperatures, suggest that these observed changes will continue and diversify as climate continues to change on the Shoshone and within the GYE. The effects of climate change on ecosystems, economies, and land use are likely to be complex and involve interacting factors that directly and indirectly affect both the physical and ecological processes.

The vulnerability of Shoshone landscapes to climate change is a function of the sensitivity of those landscapes to changes in climate, the extent to which climate changes, and the adaptive capacity of those landscapes. An example of vulnerability to climate is the relationship between fish and stream temperatures (Reiman and Isaak 2010). When temperatures exceed a certain range, the quality of habitat degrades; the greater the temperature increase, the greater the impact on salmonids. How fast and how much stream temperatures increase directly influences the impact of climate change that salmonids are exposed to. Streams that are shaded by vegetation, which helps cool stream temperatures, would have a higher adaptive capacity than unshaded streams.

Ecological responses to future climate change are challenging to quantify, especially when the changes are spatially and temporally variable with several interacting factors and stressors defining behavior. Large gradients in topography, climate, and soils (and consequently in vegetation) are found within the Shoshone. Shoshone geology varies greatly with precambrian granitic rock, Paleozoic and Mesozoic limestone, sandstone, shale, and andesite lava overlain by rhyolites diversifying soil development (Hansen 2006). Temperature varies with elevation, and seasonal precipitation varies from summer-wet regimes to winter-wet regimes. Early European settlement around the Shoshone brought mining, tie hacking and timber harvesting, and livestock grazing activities. Only 4 percent of the Shoshone has been harvested for timber; a contrast to the more widespread impacts of livestock grazing at the turn of the Twentieth Century (USDA Forest Service 2009c). The legacies of these historical disturbances affect the current condition of these landscapes (USDA Forest Service 2011a) and may influence their adaptive capacity to future climate change. In addition, human communities surrounding the Shoshone today depend upon economic activities related to tourism and recreation and upon ecosystem benefits such as water for urban and agricultural uses, thus linking the adaptive capacity of these human communities to the potential changes on the Shoshone.

In the following section, we synthesize current resource conditions and the latest scientific information about how future climate change may affect natural resources on the Shoshone and GYE. Species and ecological responses to previous and current climate change are typified by variable thresholds with nonlinear dynamics (Burkett and others 2005). Many studies have examined complex ecological behavior and project climate change effects. We synthesize the studies related to resources and natural or human influenced processes that may be vulnerable to climate change—specifically, water, vegetation, fish and wildlife, fire or insect disturbance, biochemical cycling, economic activities, and land use.

Water and Aquatic Systems

Current Conditions

The watersheds of the Shoshone provide vital water supplies for agriculture, human use, natural vegetation, and wildlife that extend outside the State of Wyoming (USDA Forest Service 2009c). The Shoshone has about 3850 miles (6200 km) of perennial streams, ~1492 miles (2401 km) of which support fish, and 310 lakes covering 10,050 acres (4067 ha) (USDA Forest Service 2008a) (Table 4). These streams and lakes provide fishery and recreation value, and are crucial for managing Yellowstone cutthroat trout, which is listed as a sensitive species in the Forest Service Rocky Mountain Region (USDA Forest Service 2009c). Groundwater supply is provided to water users through more than 600 groundwater wells covering the north, central, and southern tip of the Shoshone (Wyoming State Engineers Office 2010, http://wygl.wygisc.org/wygeolib/catalog/browse/browse.page). Surface water is supplied to users via more than 50 points of diversions that are mostly in the valleys of the northern Shoshone (Water Resource Data System points of diversion 2007, GIS data http://waterplan.state.wy.us/plan/statewide/gis/gis html). Many Shoshone watersheds are headwater basins that channel water from snow melt, rain, and glaciers primarily into the Yellowstone River and a smaller portion to the Platte River, both of which are within the Missouri Basin. Watersheds of the GYE have undergone extreme drought and wet periods over the last 700 years; wetter periods have occurred in the last century during the 1910s, 1960s, and 1970s, and drought periods occurred during the 1930s and 1950s (Graumlich and others 2003; Gray and others 2007; Kalra and others 2008). Tree ring records in the western United States and Wind River Range headwaters suggest that the Twentieth Century has been relatively wet compared to the previous 1200 years (Cook and others 2004; Watson and others 2009) (Table 4).

Table 4. Summary of water quantity and timing of annual flow conditions for the 20th Century, projections for the 21st Century, and potential consequences to ecosystem services.

	Current trend or condition over the 20th Century	Anticipated ecological response over 21st Century	Potential consequences to ecosystem services
Climate trend	• Temperature increase of 2 to 4 °F (1 to 2 °C) (especially in winter and spring) • Precipitation and snowpack decline	• Annual temperature increase range of 2 to 10 °F (1.1 to 5.5 °C) by 2100 • Annual precipitation 10% increase with wetter winters (+10%) and drier summers (-10%) (more uncertain)	
Water quantity	• Up to a 25 percent decrease in annual flows has been observed in ID, western WY and MT since 1967. • Stream flows are largely unmeasured on much of the Shoshone, and gages show no statistically significant trends.	• Peak flow increase 40 to 154 percent with 4 °F (2.2 °C) temperature increase • Summer flows decrease 30 to 62 percent with 4 °F (2.2 °C) temperature increase • Annual flows decrease 5 to 24 percent with 1 °F (0.6 °C) to 6 °F (3.4 °C) temperature increase • Drought period annual flow decrease 41 to 55 percent with 1 °F (0.6 °C) to 6 °F (3.4 °C) temperature increase and associated precipitation decreases	• Potential increase in flood magnitude with degradation of aquatic habitat • Potential loss of habitat for aquatic species from reduced streamflow • Potential reduction of 5 to 25 percent of the annual water supply for water storage • Potential reduction of up to half the annual water supply for human and agricultural use and recreation opportunities during drought • Potential increase in the use of groundwater
Timing of annual flows	• Timing ~11 days earlier in western WY, ID, and western MT since 1967 • Timing 1 to 4 weeks earlier than mid century in western U.S.	• Timing 4 to 5 weeks earlier than present with 3.6 to 7.2 °F (2 to 4 °C) temperature increase	• Altered timing of water availability for storage • Altered peak flows shifting or hindering salmonid spawning activity • Altered timing of recreational opportunities— potentially earlier and shorter for fishing, rafting, and kayaking

Stream gages on or near the Shoshone have not shown any statistically significant trend (USGS NWIS 2010, unpublished data, http://waterdata.usgs.gov/wy/nwis/rt). However, in western Wyoming, western Montana, and Idaho, an approximately 25 percent decrease in stream flow has been observed and the timing of runoff has shifted 12 days earlier since 1967 (Clark 2010) (Table 4). River basins behave similarly in that the volume of runoff is most sensitive to precipitation changes that affect snow accumulation during winter, while the timing of runoff is most affected by temperature that leads to earlier spring runoff and lower summer flows (Barnett and others 2005). Temperature increases over the latter half of the Twentieth Century have already caused stream flow timing to be one to four weeks earlier in western North America (Stewart and others 2005) (Table 4).

Almost all of the Shoshone watersheds are currently classified as in good to excellent condition (Brown and Froemke 2010; USDA Forest Service 2011a). Those watersheds in excellent condition are primarily in wilderness areas. The condition of these watersheds reflects to varying degrees past and present land use (USDA Forest Service 2011a). Generally, most are on an improving trend, and watershed concerns relate to historical uses such as heavy grazing or roading associated with motorized recreation and timber harvest. Best management practices have been put into place to address these concerns as well as concerns about wildfire activities, debris flows, and road sediment (USDA Forest Service 2008a, 2011a) (Table 4).

One additional disturbance that has recently affected many forests on the Shoshone and large areas in the western United States is bark beetle outbreaks. Bark beetle outbreaks have been observed to have variable effects on the timing and quantity of stream flow. Basin-scale changes of stream flow and timing have not been found to be consistently associated with beetle tree mortality (Lukas and Gordon 2010). However, smaller-scale observations of tree mortality from beetle outbreaks and subsequent reductions in transpiration have been observed to increase stream flow (Love 1955; Bethlahmy 1974; Potts 1984; Helie and others 2005). Stream flow was found to increase for 20 years after a beetle epidemic in Colorado (Bethlahmy 1974). Potts (1984) found a 15 percent increase in annual water yield (as did Love [1955] in Colorado), a two to three week advance in the peak hydrograph, a 10 percent increase in low flows, and little change in peak flows for the Jack Creek watershed in southwestern Montana. Troendle and Nankervis (2000) modeled the effect of spruce beetle kill on 30 and 50 percent of the spruce-fir stands in the North Platte River Basin of Colorado and Wyoming, and projected a 14 percent increase in water yield after 10 years. The authors hypothesized that the water increase would decay as vegetation grew back, but could last for 50 to 60 years. In Canada, the modeled hydrologic function of watersheds that have been infested by beetles (for example, earlier spring runoff and increased stream flow) have been projected to behave similar to clear cut areas for 40 to 60 years post-infestation (Lewis and Huggard 2010). However, these modeled effects of increased stream flow are not always consistent with observations. In the Rocky Mountains, if precipitation is below 20 inches (508 mm) per year, no changes in stream flow have been observed (MacDonald and Stednick 2003; Stednick and Jensen 2007). The potential water gains from less interception and transpiration from trees may be offset by increases in soil evaporation and increased evapotranspiration from the understory or residual trees. Additionally, the individual effects on stream flow from mountain pine beetle outbreaks that occur during precipitation and temperature variations are difficult to differentiate (Lukas and Gordon 2010). Changes to stream flow and timing due to beetle kill are not well understood at this point.

Climate Change Effects on Water Quantity and the Timing of Runoff

Globally, in snow-dominated regions, climate change is expected to reduce stream flow, ground water recharge, and reservoir storage through reduced snowpack, increased evaporation, and earlier spring runoffs with longer summers (Danielopol and others 2003; Barnett and others 2005). Temperature increases of 2 to 10 °F (1.1 to 5.5 °C) or higher are predicted to occur this century (Table 2). The timing of runoff is expected to be most dependent on winter and spring temperatures, and runoff may occur four to five weeks earlier under a 3.6 to 7.2 °F (2 to 4 °C) temperature increase in the Colorado Rocky Mountains and western United States (Baron and others 2000b; Stewart and others 2004). These timing shifts could potentially alter water availability for storage and shift salmonid spawning activity and recreational opportunities such as fishing, rafting, and kayaking (Table 4).

Several modeling studies have projected considerably reduced surface water supplies due to the effects of increasing temperatures and resulting increased evaporation, as well as precipitation reductions and extended drought. Stonefelt and others' (2000) modeling of the Upper Wind River Basin of Wyoming projected that by 2100, there could be a 100 to 154 percent increase in January to April surface runoff and a 30 to 47 percent decrease in June to August runoff with a 4 °F (2.2 °C) temperature increase and a 10 percent increase in annual precipitation. Inputting a 4 °F (2.2 °C) temperature increase and a 10 percent decrease in precipitation into the model resulted in a 40 to 75 percent January to April runoff increase, and a 50 to 62 percent decrease in June to August runoff. Gray and McCabe's (2010) modeling study for the Upper Yellowstone River of Wyoming projected that a 1 °F (0.6 °C) temperature increase by 2025 can reduce annual runoff by 11 percent below baseline levels, a 3 °F (1.7 °C) temperature increase by 2050 could reduce runoff by 15 percent, and a 4 °F (2.2 °C) temperature increase by 2100 could reduce annual runoff by 24 percent. Baseline levels were based on runoff estimates generated using tree ring precipitation and PRISM temperatures over the period 1911 to 1995. Gray and McCabe's (2010) projections for worst case scenarios of extended drought (as observed in historical records) with expected temperature increases up to 6.3 °F (3.5 °C) by 2100 resulted in 10th percentile driest annual runoff reductions of 41 percent, 45 percent, and 55 percent for 2025, 2050, and 2100, respectively, in the central Rocky Mountain region. In other words, the driest runoff levels (10th percentile) in the future may be less than half of the driest runoff levels of the historical record. Although groundwater on the Shoshone is not as well studied, globally, it is expected that high-elevation bogs (many of which occur on the northern Shoshone) may be particularly vulnerable to drying and decreased groundwater recharge (Finlayson and others 2005). The potential consequences to ecosystem services may be a degradation of aquatic habitat and a reduction of up to half of the current water supply for human and agricultural use, recreational opportunities, and aquatic wildlife (Table 4).

The projections for stream flow have large ranges that vary from 40 to 150 percent peak flow increases, 30 to 62 percent decreases in summer flow, and up to 55 percent annual flow reductions by 2100 (Table 4). Similarly, runoff projections for the Colorado River, though well studied, also have a wide range of runoff reductions (-5 to -45 percent by the 2050s) (Barnett and Pierce 2009). When the large differences for the Colorado River were examined more closely, scientists identified sources of variability, such as the spatial scale at which hydrology is modeled, the data available (or not) to calibrate the hydrological models, and the climate models used to project future climate change and the models' assumptions (Hoerling and others 2009). However, some agreements in a cross-model analysis were identified. Hoerling and others (2009) noted that the models show similar sensitivity of stream flow to precipitation changes, with a 2:1 ratio of percent change in flow to percent change in precipitation using historic data. For the Upper Colorado River, model sensitivity suggested that a 10 percent reduction in precipitation would result in a 20 percent decline in runoff. In contrast, runoff sensitivity to temperature was not as consistent across the models. Further studies are needed, particularly in areas that are not as well studied as the Colorado River.

Severe flooding events on or near the Shoshone occurred in 1918, 1923, 1963, and 1986 during June and were likely caused by snowmelt combined with severe thunderstorm activity (USGS 1989). Recent heavy precipitation and flooding events in the western United States, especially the West Coast, have been associated to atmospheric rivers. Atmospheric rivers are narrow bands of enhanced water vapor and strong atmospheric flow that originate from tropical regions of the Pacific and Atlantic oceans. These events bring extremely heavy precipitation and warmer temperatures as they make landfall in the western United States, and sometimes extend to the GYE. The water carrying capacity of atmospheric rivers is expected to increase as temperatures rise under climate change (Leung and Qian 2009). The western United States may experience rain-on-snow events that produce large runoff and flooding associated with these atmospheric rivers (Leung and Qian 2009). At the time of this report, no further specific published information was found about the effects of climate change on the magnitude and frequency of flooding in the Shoshone.

Water Quality

Current Conditions

The majority of watersheds on the Shoshone are in Wilderness Areas, and although they are largely unmeasured for water quality, the majority are classified in good condition (USDA Forest Service 2011a) (Table 5). Problems with sediments, nutrients, and toxins have been ranked very low for Shoshone watersheds (Brown and Froemke 2010). Water quality in a few watersheds is of concern due to mining activity and these watersheds are targeted for mitigation through watershed improvement plans (USDA Forest Service 2011a).

Climate Change Effects

Climate change effects could play a role in water quality degradation in several ways: (1) warmer temperatures and increased atmospheric CO_2 could affect the rates of biogeochemical processes that determine water quality (for example, algae); (2) changes in flow volumes could alter

Table 5. Summary of water quality conditions for the 20th Century, projections for the 21st Century, and potential consequences to ecosystem services.

	Current trend or condition over the 20th Century	Anticipated ecological response over 21st Century	Potential consequences to ecosystem services
Climate trend	• Temperature increase of 2 to 4 °F (1 to 2 °C) (especially in winter and spring) • Precipitation and snowpack decline	• Annual temperature increase range of 2 to 10 °F (1.1 to 5.5 °C) by 2100 • Annual precipitation 10% increase with wetter winters (+10%) and drier summers (-10%) (more uncertain)	
Water quality	The majority of Shoshone watersheds are in good condition	• Altered biogeochemical cycles • Decreased flows may increase chemical loading. • Increased disturbance may increase sedimentation.	• Potential reduction of water quality • Higher stream temperatures could potentially reduce the quality of aquatic habitat. • Potential increase of algae • Potential increased cost of water treatment

residence times and chemical loading to streams, thereby altering water quality (Arnell 1998; Murdock and others 2000); and (3) shifts in disturbance regimes (for example, increased fire) caused by a warmer, drier climate may alter water quality indirectly by increasing sediment loads (Meyer and others 1992). Flanagan and others (2003) compared temperature and lakes occupying latitudes ranging from 40 to 80°, and suggested that the warmer temperatures at lower latitudes could cause increased algal productivity. The effects from increased atmospheric CO_2 have been observed to alter algae and plant dynamics in global oceans (Feely and others 2004). Increased temperatures have also been found to increase algae growth and, therefore, the need for water treatment (Koschel 2010). Algae causes problems in the drinking water supply in reservoirs such as toxicity, water deoxygenation, odor, and clogged systems (Koschel 2010). Several algae types have already been found in Colorado reservoirs, most commonly in the reservoirs that allow motorized watercraft, and could cause a public health hazard under a climate with warmer temperatures and increased drought (Koschel 2010). A longer growing season, glacial retreat, and warmer water temperatures are expected to increase sediment fluxes and concentrations, affecting the chemical, mineral, and nutrient status of streams and lakes and having deleterious effects on the food chain of western North America (Moore and others 2009). Nitrate increases in Colorado high-elevation streams has occurred and is thought to be largely due to increased glacial melt water flushing microbially rich sediments (Baron and others 2009). Water quality degradation may exceed thresholds of ecosystem tolerance during extreme events such as storms, drought, or extended periods of elevated temperatures and increased fire (Murdoch and others 2000). At the time of this report, no studies on the Shoshone have been found that link future climate change with water quality changes. However, the potential consequences to water quality may be higher temperatures that reduce the quality of aquatic habitat and increase the potential for higher amounts of algae, as well as the projected increase in disturbance that would cause more sedimentation to occur more frequently (Table 5).

Glaciers

Current Condition

Glacial retreat and advance for the Pinedale and Bull Lake glaciers in YNP and Teton National Park (TNP) has been highly variable spatially and temporally from about 150,000 to 12,000 years ago (Liciardi and Pierce 2008). Since the Little Ice Age (1300 to 1850), glaciers in western North America have retreated in response to general warming trends (Moore and others 2009). Wyoming contributes approximately 6 percent of total glacial area in the conterminous United States (http://www.glaciers.pdx.edu/), a large fraction of which is found on the Shoshone in the Wind River Range (Cheesebrough 2009) (Figure 18). The Wind River Range contains 7 of the 10 largest glaciers

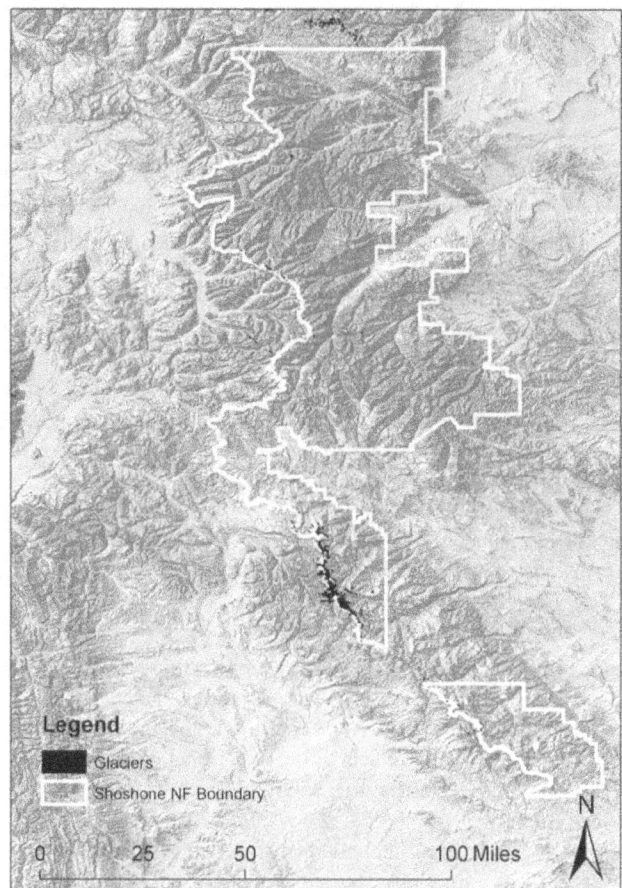

Figure 18. Glacier distribution, 2005. Source: http://glaciers.us/Downloads.

in the U.S. Rocky Mountains (Oswald and Wohl 2008). Recent glacial mass reductions of 25 percent have been observed since 1985 (Cheesbrough and others 2009), and there was a loss of 0.53 mi³ (0.86 km³) of glacial ice volume from 1966 to 2001 (Bell 2009). Pochop and others (1990) reported evidence that the two largest glaciers in the Wind Rivers have receded in the past 50 years and are continuing to do so. More recently, a jökulhlaup (a type of outburst flood that originates from melt water ponded by glacial ice) that burst from the Grasshopper Glacier provides indirect evidence of glacial melt (Oswald and Wohl 2008).

Glacier retreat can temporarily mitigate reductions in runoff volume. Cheesbrough and others (2009) found that the 25 percent reduction of glacial mass that has occurred since 1985 has been contributing 4 to 10 percent of July to October stream flow in the Wind River Range (Table 6). And the 0.53 mi³ (0.86 km³) loss of glacial ice that occurred from 1966 to 2001 may have contributed +6 to +25 percent to annual stream flow and 35 to 40 percent of late summer flow (Table 6). However, changes in stream flow may also be attributed to precipitation changes (Graumlich and others 2003), making it difficult to discern precise stream flow increases from glacial melt.

Table 6. Summary of glacier conditions for the 20th Century, projections for the 21st Century, and potential consequences to ecosystem services.

	Current trend or condition over the 20th Century	Anticipated ecological response over 21st Century	Potential consequences to ecosystem services
Climate trend	• Temperature increase of 2 to 4 °F (1 to 2 °C) (especially in winter and spring) • Precipitation and snowpack decline	• Annual temperature increase range of 2 to 10 °F (1.1 to 5.5 °C) by 2100 • Annual precipitation 10% increase with wetter winters (+10%) and drier summers (-10%) (more uncertain)	
Glaciers	• Large reduction (~25 percent) since mid century in Wind River Range • Glacial melt may contribute 4 to 25 percent of annual flows and 35 to 40 percent of late summer flow in the Wind River Range	• Potential for complete glacier loss before mid century with 4.5 °F (2.5 °C) annual temperature increase • Reductions in streamflow with eventual loss of glaciers • Potential increase of stream temperatures as glaciers disappear	• Existing glaciers may help mitigate reductions in water supply during summer • Potential reductions in summer streamflow as glaciers disappear • Potential loss of micro-site terrestrial habitat adjacent to glaciers • Potential shift in suitability of aquatic thermal habitat

Climate Change Effects on Glaciers

The response of glaciers to future climate change is a complex interaction among temperature, precipitation, and solar radiation (Hall and Fagre 2003). Increased winter precipitation (as projected for the Shoshone during winter) would result in greater accumulation but only if winter temperatures are low enough to create snow (Hall and Fagre 2003). Summer temperature has been found to explain 92 percent of glacier change in Glacier National Park (GNP), mostly by its direct effect on ablation (the erosive process of melting and evaporation by which a glacier is reduced) and the associated increase in solar radiation (Hall and Fagre 2003). However, Hall and Fagre (2003) modeled glacial loss in GNP under a doubling of CO_2 and found that winter precipitation did not buffer glacial loss. On the contrary, the modeled summer temperature increase of 4.5 °F (2.5 °C) by 2050 resulted in the complete loss of glaciers by 2030 (Hall and Fagre 2003).

The local effect of climate change on glaciers on the Shoshone will vary according to glacier elevation, size, shape, slope/aspect position, and local monthly temperature and precipitation (Hall and Fagre 2003; Granshaw and Fountain 2006). The elevation of a glacier plays a role in the location of its equilibrium line (the point at which on either side the accumulation and ablation zones are equal in area) (Granshaw and Fountain 2006). Larger glaciers are less susceptible to loss in the near-term, and the shape of the glacier influences the dynamics between the ablation and accumulation zones.

Overall, there is consensus that western U.S. glaciers will continue to retreat in the next 100 years (Hall and Fagre 2003; Christensen and others 2007; Moore and others 2009). Even though glacial loss affects a relatively small portion of the landscape, the effects are far reaching: downstream aquatic habitats and water quality may be degraded by increased stream temperatures and sediment; and summer stream flow may be reduced, thereby altering the reliability of water resources for human communities (Burkett and others 2005; Moore and others 2009). However, future stream flow reductions could be partially mitigated by glacier melt (while glaciers are present). The potential consequences to ecosystem services may be a temporary increase in summer stream flow followed by a reduction as glaciers disappear, terrestrial habitat that is near glaciers could be lost, and the suitability of aquatic thermal habitat near glaciers will likely shift as glaciers disappear (Table 6).

Snow

Current Conditions

Most of the western United States has already experienced declines in snowpack that may be associated with warming, earlier snowmelt, and more precipitation falling as rain instead of snow (Naftz and others 2002; Regonda and others 2004; Mote and others 2005; Stewart and others 2005; Knowles and others 2006). Since the 1940s, a moderate warming trend has shifted snowmelt 10 to 28 days

Table 7. Summary of snow conditions for the 20th Century, projections for the 21st Century, and potential consequences to ecosystem services.

	Current trend or condition over the 20th Century	Anticipated ecological response over 21st Century	Potential consequences to ecosystem services
Climate trend	• Temperature increase of 2 to 4 °F (1 to 2 °C) (especially in winter and spring) • Precipitation and snowpack decline	• Annual temperature increase range of 2 to 10 °F (1.1 to 5.5 °C) by 2100 • Annual precipitation 10% increase with wetter winters (+10%) and drier summers (-10%) (more uncertain)	
Snow	• Declining snowpack in the western U.S. • Western U.S. snowmelt 10 to 28 days earlier since mid 20th Century	• 30 to 50 percent annual snowpack loss with 9 °F (5 °C) temperature increase in the Colorado River Basin	• Potentially less annual water supply stored as snow and earlier release of stream flows for storage • Potential loss of winter habitat for snow-dependent wildlife • Potential reductions of snow recreation opportunities for skiing, snow shoeing, and snow mobiling, especially at lower elevations

earlier in western North America (Regonda and others 2004; Stewart and others 2005) (Table 7).

Windstorm events in Arizona, Utah, and western Colorado have recently been observed to deposit a layer of dust on snowpack in Colorado and southern Wyoming that change hydrologic function (Rhoades and others 2010). The dust increases solar radiation absorption, accelerating snow melt, causing an earlier runoff, and altering water chemistry (Painter and others 2007, 2010; Neff and others 2008; Steltzer and others 2009; Rhoades and others 2010). Dust-on-snow events have largely impacted the Colorado Rocky Mountains, but at this time, no information has been found about dust-on-snow events of this magnitude in the GYE.

Climate Change Effects on Snow

In the near-term, increased winter precipitation could increase snowpack in the northwestern United States (Whitlock and others 2003)[1]. While this has been simulated up to 2059, if temperatures continue to increase, a threshold will eventually be crossed where most winter precipitation will fall as rain instead of snow (Whitlock and others 2003). Baron and others (2000a) simulated a doubling of CO_2 with

a concurrent 7 °F (4 °C) temperature increase at a high-altitude watershed (9800 to 13,000 ft [2990 to 3965 m]) in Rocky Mountain National Park, Colorado. Under those conditions, simulated snowpack was reduced by 50 percent and runoff began four to five weeks earlier (Baron and others 2000a). Under future climate projections for the Shoshone, snowfall will likely shift to rainfall at progressively higher elevations, and snowmelt will continually start earlier in the year as temperatures warm (Ray and others 2008). A modeling study for the Colorado River Basin showed that areas above 8200 ft (2500 m) elevation had less snow loss compared to areas below 8200 ft (2500 m) by the year 2050 (Ray and others 2008). A 30 to 50 percent reduction in snowpack was projected at elevations above 8200 ft (2500 m) with a 9 °F (5 °C) temperature increase by the year 2100 (Ray and others 2008). The highest elevations of the Shoshone may be buffered from snowpack loss if results from the Colorado study can be extended to Wyoming. However, the overall consequences to ecosystem services may be: a reduced annual water supply being stored as snow, an earlier release of stream flow for water storage, a loss of winter habitat for snow-dependent wildlife, and reduced snow recreation opportunities, especially at lower elevations (Table 7).

---

[1] Whitlock and others (2003) used climate data from HADCM2 HCGSa for the period 2050-2059, as found in Mitchell and Johns (1997).

Table 8. Summary of wetland conditions for the 20th Century, projections for the 21st Century, and potential consequences to ecosystem services.

	Current trend or condition over the 20th Century	Anticipated ecological response over 21st Century	Potential consequences to ecosystem services
Climate trend	• Temperature increase of 2 to 4 °F (1 to 2 °C) (especially in winter and spring) • Precipitation and snowpack decline	• Annual temperature increase range of 2 to 10 °F (1.1 to 5.5 °C) by 2100 • Annual precipitation 10% increase with wetter winters (+10%) and drier summers (-10%) (more uncertain)	
Wetlands	• Willow communities on the Shoshone have experienced an increase in conifer encroachment	• Increased potential for wetland desiccation globally	• Potential reduction or loss of wetlands • Potential loss of habitat for many species using or dependent on wetlands • Potential alteration in local hydrology because of changes to, or disappearance of, wetlands

Wetlands

Current Condition

Wetlands occupy a small percentage of the Shoshone but serve important ecological functions such as increasing biodiversity, providing important spawning grounds, supporting a wide variety of biota, serving as natural flood control, cleansing and replenishing groundwater, cleansing agricultural and urban runoff, and offering recreation and aesthetic value (Copeland and others 2010). The wetlands in the Beartooth Mountains of the northern Shoshone have high botanical significance, representing the widest known array of wetland fen[2] types in Wyoming, and are among the highest known concentrations of fen sites and rare plant species in Wyoming (Heidel and Rodemaker 2008). In 1961, a permanently frozen peat deposit in the Northern Shoshone Beartooth Mountains was reported as a very rare occurrence of permafrost at that latitude, indicating that climate conditions and insulating cover were sufficient to support permafrost at that time (Pierce 1961).

Some Shoshone wetlands were affected by tie hacking (especially at high elevations), water diversions (at low elevations), and grazing (especially at lower elevations) at the turn of the Twentieth Century. These effects may have decreased the abundance of some willow communities and favored succession to conifers within riparian areas (Table 8). Analysis of aerial photos (1937 to 1997) has documented changes to some riparian areas from livestock grazing, and encroachment by conifers that has caused the decline of deciduous aspen (*Populus tremuloides*) and willow vegetation (USDA Forest Service 2009b).

Climate Change Effects on Wetlands

Globally, wetlands are expected to decline in area over the next century as they are extremely vulnerable to climate change (IPCC 2007b). Warmer temperatures will increase evaporation, leading to an increased chance of wetland desiccation, as well as altering wetland species communities and nutrient cycling, increasing decomposition, and potentially creating a C source (Burkett and Kusler 2000). Lower-elevation wetlands of Wyoming outside the Shoshone have been found to be the most affected by land use, are classified in the poorest condition, and are most vulnerable to future changes (Copeland and others 2010). Wetlands are very sensitive to changes in precipitation, especially if precipitation is the major source of water as opposed to groundwater (Winter 2000). At the time of this report, no published information was found on groundwater and climate change on the Shoshone. However, earlier snow melt, reduced summer precipitation, and longer growing seasons will likely cause reduced water inputs and lowering of water tables in wetlands, especially during late summer (Erwin 2009). The potential consequences to the Shoshone wetlands

---

[2] Fens are peat forming wetlands that receive their nutrients from sources other than precipitation. Fens are less acidic and have high nutrient contents that can support diverse plant and animal communities.

Table 9. Paleo-historic vegetation of the Wind River Range and YNP (Fall and others 2005; Whitlock 1993).

	14,000 to 11,500 BP	11,500 to 10,500 BP	10,500 to 9500 BP	9500 to 5000 BP	5000 to 3000 BP	3000 BP to present
YNP area **6500 to 9200 ft (2000 to 2800 m) elevation**	Alpine meadow, shrub (grass, herb, birch, juniper)	Spruce parkland (Englemann spruce, fir, whitebark pine)	Spruce-fir-pine forest	Lodgepole pine forest with Douglas-fir, aspen	Lodgepole pine forest, increasing spruce, fir, grass; decreasing Douglas-fir	
Wind River Range **9800 ft (3000 m) elevation**	Alpine tundra (juniper)	Mixed conifer forest (pine, fir, spruce)				Whitebark pine parkland

that will likely face higher temperatures may be a reduction or loss of these habitats and the associated species dependent upon them, as well as altered hydrology if these habitats disappear (Table 8).

Vegetation

Paleo-Historic and Current Vegetation

Plant species distributions and compositions on the Shoshone and the GYE have varied greatly for thousands of years (Table 9). Paleo-ecological studies for the GYE show that individual species respond to climate change predominately by shifting ranges (Whitlock and Bartlein 1993). Pollen records for the Wind River Range, Grand Teton National Forest and YNP (study site locations in Figure 2) show that cooler conditions between ~14,000 BP

and ~11,500 BP caused the upper tree line of birch (*Betula* spp.) and juniper (*Juniperus* spp.) species to be about 1000 ft (305 m) lower than present (below 9200 ft [2800 m] elevation). Warmer temperatures and wetter conditions from ~11,500 BP to ~10,500 BP allowed the presence of spruce (*Picea* spp.), fir (*Abies* spp.), and whitebark pine (*Pinus albicaulis*) in the northern and southern Yellowstone regions and in the Wind River Range. Lodgepole pine (*Pinus contorta*) appeared and persisted around 10,500 BP as temperatures continued to increase. Douglas-fir (*Pseudotseuga menziesii*) and poplar (*Populus* spp.) were present in lodgepole pine-dominated forests in the southern Yellowstone region from ~9500 to ~5000 BP under warmer and drier conditions. Mixed forests of spruce, fir, and pine have been present for the last ~5000 years, and the modern tree-line position occupied by whitebark pine at around 10,500 ft (3200 m)

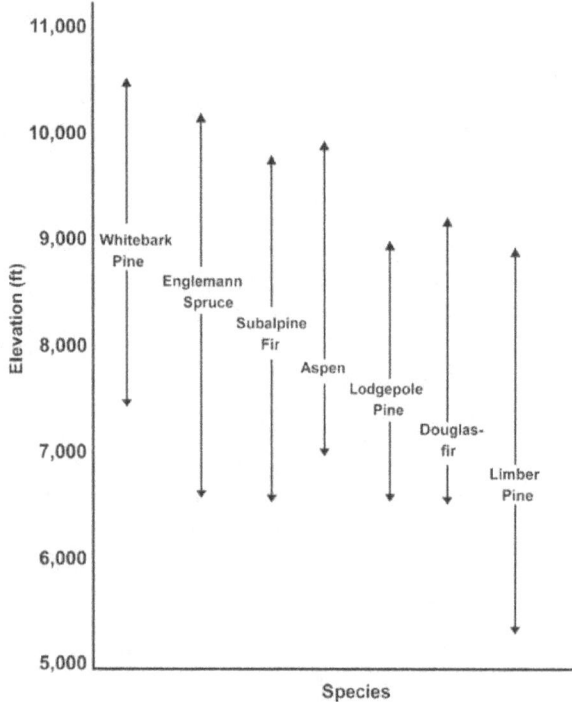

Figure 19. Shoshone tree species elevation ranges.

elevation was established ~ 3000 years ago (Whitlock 1993; Fall and others 1995) (Table 9).

The current vegetation of the Shoshone varies widely due to variations in elevation, aspect, latitude, climate, site conditions, and past disturbances (Figure 19) (USDA Forest Service 2009b). The Shoshone lies in the Yellowstone Highlands section of the Southern Rocky Mountain Steppe-Open Woodland-Coniferous Forest-Alpine Meadow Province (McNab and others 2005). This landscape includes rugged mountains with glacially formed cirques, broad valleys, and rounded ridges with rocks of volcanic origin. About 60 percent of the Shoshone's rugged landscape is covered by trees, about 30 percent is dominated by grasses and forbs, and about 10 percent is rock and ice at the highest elevations. Tree cover in the montane and subalpine zones is between about 6000 ft (1829 m) and about 10,500 ft (3200 m) elevation and comprises about 57 million tons (63 million metric tons) of live biomass (Menlove 2008).

Climate Change Effects on Vegetation

Climate has influenced the patterns of vegetation distributions and their fluctuation in the GYE over long time periods. The ongoing and rapid rates of climate change that are expected in the next 100 years will likely outpace post-glacial rates since 20,000 BP and will likely have far reaching effects on future biogeography (Whitlock and others 2003). Some species may benefit from warmer temperatures and longer growing seasons, other species may adapt to new conditions or migrate to a more suitable environment, and some may go extinct (Aitkin 2008). Although it is difficult to predict how plant communities will develop and interact under climate change, the future dynamics of vegetation communities will likely be complex and determined by species dispersal rates, individual species response to environmental conditions, availability of suitable recruitment sites (for example, suitable soil depth or available habitat), disturbance regime (for example, fire, wind, or insects), nutrient availability, microclimate, and precipitation and temperature (Whitlock and Bartlein 1993; Bartlein and others 1998; Shafer and others 2001).

Alpine Zone Vegetation

Current Conditions

Alpine areas comprise 25 percent (625,000 acres or 252,930 ha) of the Shoshone (Table 10). These are high-biodiversity areas with short growing seasons and rugged or rocky topography that host shrubs, grass, and forb species. Over 400 of the worldwide 8000 to 10,000 species of alpine flora occur on the Beartooth Plateau that extends into the northern Shoshone (Kripps and Eddington 2005). Several of these 400 species are considered rare taxa (for example, the insectivorious English sundew [*drosera anglica*], Alpine arnica [*Arnica angustifolia* ssp. *Tomentosa*], and White arctic whitlow-grass [*Draba fladnizensis* var. *pattersonii*]).

It is uncertain whether other environmental factors limit tree line migration into alpine areas on the Shoshone (Table 10). On the northern Shoshone Beartooth Plateau, no evidence was found of whitebark pine invasions into alpine

meadows above its current ecotone (Mellman-Brown 2002). However, alpine vegetation has been observed to shift upward in elevation (Swiss Alps, Walther and others 2005; Italian Alps, Cannone and others 2007). Rocky Mountain studies have found a 60-ft (20-m) advance in tree line since 1938 on the west side of Pikes Peak in Colorado (Freiden 2010), episodic tree line advancement during the 1950s and 1960s in Rocky Mountain National Park (Hessl and Baker 1997), and no tree line advance but increased tree line density and fragmentation in Glacier National Park (Klasner and Fagre 2002) (fragmentation is defined here as the disconnection of areas from one another within a landscape or ecosystem [Hobbs and others 2008]). The inconsistency of tree line advance in these areas may be due to inertia (slow tree establishment, growth, and reproduction rates), disturbance, drought, and nutrient or soil limitations (Mellman-Brown 2002; Dullinger and others 2004; Malanson and others 2007; Smith and others 2009).

Climate Change Effects on Alpine Zone Vegetation

Alpine areas are expected to undergo the greatest amount of warming (Christensen and others 2007) and are sensitive to climate change (Christensen and others 2007). While Christensen and others (2007) reported that high elevations are expected to undergo the greatest amount of warming, Pepin and Lundquist (2008) reported that, based on observed Twentieth Century temperature trends, there has been no simplistic elevational increase in warming rates globally. Pepin and Lundquist (2008) documented the most rapid temperature trends at the annual 0 °C isotherm (the line where mean annual temperature is 32 °F) due to snow-ice feedback; and they suggested that ecosystems near the isotherm in the mid latitudes beyond the tropics are at increased risk from accelerated warming. The dynamics of tree line change will be influenced by the nature of the spatial changes in temperature across the higher elevations.

Globally, alpine vegetation extent is expected to decrease and fragment because temperatures may warm at higher rates than at lower elevations (Christensen and others 2007). Alpine areas are projected to be reduced or eliminated by the advancement of the tree line (Romme and Turner 1991; Bachelet and others 2001; Ashton 2010) (Table 10). The potential consequences to ecosystem services include a decline in alpine habitat with a potential for high-elevation refugia to develop dynamic and novel plant communities (Table 10). Grace and others (2002) suggested that tree line could be expected to advance vertically by 2100 ft (640 m) by the year 2100 with a future temperature increase of 7.2 to 9 °F (4 to 5 °C) in the alpine areas of northern Europe. Given the potentially large magnitude of temperature increase and the rapid rate of potential upslope migration, rare species, those with low dispersal rates, and those with narrow bioclimatic niches may be affected negatively (Shafer and others 2001). However, adaptable species may survive in refugia sites that develop as climate changes (Noss 2001; Ashcroft 2010). Within YNP and Grand Teton National Park, Schrag and others (2008) found a complex response of tree-line conifer

Table 10. Summary of vegetation conditions for the 20th Century, projections for the 21st Century, and potential consequences to ecosystem services.

	Current trend or condition over the 20th Century	Anticipated ecological response over 21st Century	Potential consequences to ecosystem services
Climate trend	• Temperature increase of 2 to 4 °F (1 to 2 °C) (especially in winter and spring) • Precipitation and snowpack decline	• Annual temperature increase range of 2 to 10 °F (1.1 to 5.5 °C) by 2100 • Annual precipitation 10% increase with wetter winters (+10%) and drier summers (-10%) (more uncertain)	
Vegetation	• Alpine areas comprise 25 percent or 625,000 acres (252,930 ha) of the Shoshone	• Decreased alpine vegetation area extent and increased fragmentation	• Potential decline or extirpation of alpine habitat
	• Episodic tree line advance in southern Rocky Mountains • Tree line dynamics largely unknown on Shoshone	• Tree line advance to higher elevations of Shoshone that is affected by moisture availability	• Potential for higher-elevation refugia for dynamic and novel combinations of plant species
	• Whitebark pine decline in GYE	• Whitebark pine retreats from lower-elevation range and either marginally exists at highest elevations of the Shoshone or is extirpated	• Potential reduction in or loss of the keystone species whitebark pine that is used by wildlife
	• Aspen decline in early 2000s in parts of North America, with aspen expansion in some areas of Rocky Mountains	• Aspen suitable climate moves upward in elevation on Shoshone	• Potential loss of low-elevation habitat associated with aspen
	• Montane lower-elevation species expanding to lower elevations on Shohone	• Douglas-fir, lodgepole pine expand range up in elevation and vacate lower elevations	• Potential reduction or loss of low-elevation habitat associated with Douglas-fir and lodgepole pine, but increase in higher-elevation associated habitat
	• Grass and sagebrush experiencing conifer encroachment on Shoshone	• Expansion of grass and sagebrush upward in elevation	• Potential increased grazing opportunities as grasslands expand upward in elevation

USDA Forest Service RMRS-GTR-264. 2012.

species to modeled changes in future temperature and precipitation. Under a scenario with a temperature increase and a scenario with temperature and precipitation increases, areas occupied by each tree species (whitebark pine, subalpine fir, and Engelmann spruce) decreased. Changes in the spatial distribution of tree line conifers were coupled with relative moisture, which identified the importance of moisture availability to tree line composition and structure.

Subalpine Zone Vegetation

Current Conditions

The subalpine zone (above 9000 to 10,500 ft or 2743 to 3200 m) on the Shoshone hosts whitebark pine at the upper edges of tree line and mixes with subalpine fir, Engelmann spruce, and lodgepole pine at lower elevations, with minor occurrences of aspen and willow on moister sites (USDA Forest Service 2009b).

Whitebark pine is a keystone species of the subalpine zone of the Rocky Mountains of Wyoming, Montana, Idaho, and Alberta (Canada) that enhances biodiversity, regulates watershed function, and is an important ecosystem component involving Clark's nutcracker (*Nucifraga columbiana*), red squirrel (*Tamiasciurus hudsonicus*), black bear (*Ursus americanus*), and grizzly bear (*Ursus arctos horribilis*) (Ellison and others 2005; Tomback and Resler 2007). Whitebark pine population decrease has been observed over the last 40 years (Kendall and Keane 2001), and is thought to be due to the spread of white pine blister rust (*Cronartium ribicola*), fire suppression, and mountain pine beetle (*Dendroctonus ponderosae*) outbreaks (Keane and Arno 1993; Koteen 2002; Gibson 2006) (Table 10). The decline of whitebark pine may be beyond historic observations of beetle outbreaks during the 1930s and 1970s in the GYE (Logan and others 2010) (Table 10). The rate of whitebark pine regeneration has recently been increasing in Montana, Idaho, and Oregon, especially where widespread mortality from mountain pine beetle infestations provided suitable conditions for regeneration (Larson and Kipfmueller 2010). However, restoration projects in central-eastern Idaho and western Montana have not produced significant whitebark pine regeneration due to white pine blister rust mortality of seed sources (Keane and Parsons 2010).

Climate Change Effects on Subalpine Zone Vegetation

The effect of climate change on whitebark pine may not be clear in the short term due to inertia and the likely involvement of complex interacting factors. Warmer temperatures may limit the available habitat, especially at lower elevations, and it is projected that whitebark pine populations will continue to decline (Romme and Turner 1991; Bartlein and others 1997; Schrag and others 2008) (Table 10). Growth and regeneration could be enhanced by longer and warmer growing seasons, increased precipitation, and higher atmospheric CO_2, but it could inhibited by drought and heat stress, species competition, increased spread of white pine blister rust, and mountain pine beetle infestations under warmer temperatures and wetter winters (Romme and Turner 1991;

Bartlein and others 1997; Koteen 2002; Schrag and others 2008). Climate envelope modeling by the USDA Forest Service (http://forest.moscowfsl.wsu.edu/climate/species/) using the A2 scenario projects that by 2090, a temperature increase of 9.1 °F (5.1 °C) would cause whitebark pine suitable climate to contract to the highest elevation areas in the northern Shoshone and GYE or be extirpated (Table 10). Loehman and others' (2010) modeling study indicated that climate changes may significantly impact whitebark pines in Glacier National Park through the indirect mechanisms of altered distributions of competing tree species and increased fire frequency and fire size.

Montane Zone Vegetation

Current Conditions

Lower-elevation forest (6000 to 9000 ft [1829 to 2743 m]) montane zone species are characterized by Douglas-fir, lodgepole pine, and limber pine (*Pinus flexilis*) (Steele and others 1981) with minor occurrences of aspen in wetter areas (USDA Forest Service 2009b) (Figure 19). Subalpine species (whitebark pine, subalpine fir, aspen, and Englemann spruce) can extend down into the montane zone, occuring in both the montane and subalpine zones. Dominant montane understory forest plant species vary greatly with environmental conditions. Among the species used to distinguish the habitat types are snowberry (*Symphoricarpos albus*), common juniper (*Juniperus communis*), hollyleaved barberry (*Mahonia aquifolium*), russet buffaloberry (*Shepherdia canadensis)*, dwarf huckleberry (*Gaylusssacia dumosa*), heartleaf arnica (*Arnica cordifolia*), and graminoids Idaho fescue (*Festuca idahoensis*) and Ross' sedge (*Carex rossii*) (USDA Forest Service 2009b).

Climate Change Effects on Montane Zone Vegetation

The montane lower-elevation species composition may be altered by future climate change (Romme and Turner 1991; Bartlein and others 1997; Shafer and others 2001). Species such as Douglas-fir and lodgepole pine may expand in range, dominating not only their current range but also higher elevations (Bartlein and others 1998) (Table 10). Lower tree line may move downslope in response to greater winter precipitation (Romme and Turner 1991) but could eventually retreat to higher elevations when temperature increases prohibit tree establishment and growth (Shafer and others 2001). Upper-elevation species occupying the lower end of their environmental tolerance are predicted to abandon lower elevations, causing a shift in community structure and function (Romme and Turner 1991; Bachelet and others 2003; Rehfeldt and others 2009).

Aspen

Current Conditions

Aspen on the Shoshone occupy about 22,000 acres (8903 ha) or 0.9 percent, spanning elevations from about 7000 to 10,000 ft elevation (2135 to 3050 m). The species is most prevalent on the south end of the Shoshone (USDA Forest Service 2009b), which is thought to be due to the presence of clay soils and areas of moisture collection in the Wind River Mountains (K. Houston, personal communication, 2011). Aspen in the western United States are valued for their high biodiversity, forage production, water yield regulation, nutrient cycling, and aesthetic value (McCool 2001; LaMalfa and Ryel 2008; Morelli and Carr 2011). Some aspen communities throughout North America have been declining in the latter half of the Twentieth Century, primarily due to fire suppression, conifer encroachment, excessive ungulate grazing, insects, fungal pathogens, and drought (Romme and others 1995; Chong and others 2001; Hogg and others 2002, 2008; Krishnan and others 2006; Hollenbeck and Ripple 2007; Rehfeldt and others 2009; Durham and Marlow 2010; Morelli and Carr 2011) (Table 10). Until recently, some areas of the Rocky Mountains have experienced an expansion in aspen regeneration and coverage extent at a local scale (western Colorado, Manier and Laven 2002; western Wyoming, Hessl and Graumlich 2002). Recent aspen mortality episodes from 2000 to 2003 in North America have been attributed to drought (Hogg and others 2008; Rehfeldt and others 2009). Aspen growth has been shown to have variable sensitivity to temperature and precipitation in YNP (Jules and others 2010). Factors that can contribute to aspen success in the United States are:

- precipitation between 15 and 40 inches (381 to 1018 mm);
- mild winters and warm, wet summers (Brown and others 2006);
- fine, well-drained soils that are high in organic matter derived from igneous rock with water tables 2 to 8 ft (0.6 to 2.5 m) deep (Perala 1990);
- lack of conifer competition;
- enhanced water use efficiency and photosynthesis from higher atmospheric CO_2 levels (Lindroth and others 1993);
- less browsing pressure by elk due to wolf predation in YNP (Halofsky and Ripple 2008); and
- reductions in elk browsing from hunting or feeding of elk in the YNP area (Hessl and Graumlich 2002).

Climate Change Effects on Aspen

One bioclimate modeling study has projected that aspen populations are likely to decline in the future under expected changes in climate (Rehfeldt and others 2009). Rehfeldt and others (2009) projected that future reduction of potential aspen distributions would largely be due to dryness and temperature warming. However, the bioclimate model did not take into account increasing atmospheric CO_2 concentrations, which have been experimentally shown to increase aspen growth in Wisconsin (Isebrands and others 2001), or other factors that may influence aspen distribution such as soils, disturbance regime, or species competition. However, Rehfeldt and others' (2009) projections that considered future temperature and precipitation showed an upslope migration of aspen and a reduction in potentially suitable habitat at higher elevation on the Shoshone. By 2100, the upper elevation of the mid and southern Shoshone was one

of the few potential climatically suitable aspen refugia left in the western United States as aspen migrated up to 3280 ft (1000 m) upslope and vacated up to 50 percent of its current distribution in the western United States (Rehfeldt and others 2009) (Table 10).

Grass and Sagebrush

Current Conditions

Grasslands on the Shoshone cover over 700,000 acres (283,279 ha), much of which occurs below ~6500 ft (1982 m) elevation, but also includes forest openings and alpine areas of higher elevations (USDA Forest Service 2009b). These grasslands are dominated by Idaho fescue (*Festuca idahoensis*), bluebunch wheatgrass (*Pseudoroegneria spicata*), sandberg bluegrass (*Poa secunda*), and june grass (*Koelaria* spp.). Grasses are sometimes mixed with sagebrush below the montane zone in the foothills. Sagebrush occupies over 30,000 acres (1240 ha) of the Shoshone, with *Artemesia* spp. dominating most of these areas that occur on deeper more developed soils (Tweit and Houston 1980). Sagebrush is sometimes mixed with grass in forest openings at lower elevations and in areas of limited moisture, disturbance, or harsh environmental conditions (USDA Forest Service 2009b). Grasslands and sagebrush are largely constrained by water availability, temperature, nutrients, soil, and disturbance (Parton and others 1994; Polley and others 1997). Grass and sagebrush dominate Shoshone elevations below 6500 ft (1982 m) but also occur at higher elevation where trees are precluded due to moisture limitation, thin soils, wind, and/or disturbance (Tweit and Houston 1980; USDA Forest Service 2009b). Areas of grass and sagebrush have been impacted by Euro-American settlement, land use, grazing, fire suppression, and invasive species, especially at lower elevations (Meyer and others 2006; USDA Forest Service 2009b).

Recently, conifer invasion into sagebrush and grasslands has been increasing on the Shoshone (USDA Forest Service 2009c) (Table 10). Powell and Hansen (2007) reported conifer cover increase in transects that were recently burned or logged over the 1971 to 1999 period, suggesting that the structure and composition of conifer-grass ecotones in the GYE are rapidly changing. A 10-fold juniper expansion into sagebrush has been observed in eastern Oregon (Rowland and others 2008), which has experienced a climate regime similar to low elevations on the Shoshone. The explicit cause for this conifer increase and any potential interaction with the current bark beetle outbreak remains to be studied.

Climate Change Effects on Grasslands and Sagebrush

Information about the effects of climate change on grasslands and sagebrush on the Shoshone is limited. However, the effects of increased CO_2 have been shown to particularly favor sagebrush increase over grass in the Great Plains (Polley 1997; Morgan and others 2007). Improved water use efficiency from higher atmospheric CO_2 concentrations available for trees may also facilitate the expansion of conifers (Powell and Hansen 2007). Tree invasion may continue or increase on the Shoshone (Bachelet and others 2001, 2003) in the short term, while water availability is adequate to support conifers. But conifer expansion into grass and sagebrush at lower elevations could eventually be reversed when temperature increases and moisture limitations at the forest-grassland ecotone prohibit tree establishment and growth (Shafer and others 2001), allowing grass and sagebrush to expand upward in elevation (Table 10). Big sagebrush (*Artemisia tridentata*) distribution in the western United States is projected to decrease in the southern portion of its range (New Mexico, Arizona, Colorado, Utah, and Nevada), and increase in the northern portion of its range (Montana) by the end of the Twenty-First Century (Schlaepfer and others 2011). Projections for big sagebrush in the lower elevations of the GYE and Shoshone indicated that a contraction may occur, while higher elevations could see some expansion (Schlaepfer and others 2011) (Table 10). A potential consequence to ecosystem services, if moisture limitations are a factor in the future, may be the eventual expansion of grasslands to higher elevations that could increase the area available for grazing (Table 10).

Invasive Species

Invasives are introduced species to ecosystems that harm the environment, economy, or human health (NISIC 2010). Invasive species can destroy or degrade ecosystem health by reducing native species richness, biodiversity, and productivity (DiTomaso 2000), and they can degrade forage for wildlife and livestock grazing (USDA Forest Service 2011a). Millions of acres of U.S. land and water have been affected by thousands of invasive plants, aquatic organisms, pests, and pathogens that have caused major disruptions to ecosystem function (NISIC 2010).

Current Conditions

Statewide, Wyoming's forests, rangelands, and aquatic systems are threatened by the expansion of 30 invasive plant species (USDA 2010), 3 mollusk species (USGS 2010), 9 fish species (USGS 2010; Wyoming Game and Fish 2010), and 3 pathogens.

On the Shoshone, 5000 to 6000 acres (2023 to 2428 ha) have been impacted by invasive populations of knapweeds (*Centaurea*), thistles (*Cirsium*), leafy spurge (*Euphorbia esula)*, oxeye daisy (*Leucanthemum vulgare*), whitetop (*Lepidium draba*), houndstongue (*Cynoglossum officinale*), common tansy (*Tanacetum vulgare*), cheatgrass (*Bromus tectorum*), and toadflax (*Linaria vulgaris*) (USDA Forest Service 2011a) (Table 11). White pine blister rust (*Cronartium ribicola*) affects white and limber pine trees on the Shoshone. Aquatic nuisances—whirling disease (*Myxobolus cerebralis*), New Zealand mudsnails (*Potamopyrgus antipodarum)*, Eurasian watermilfoil (*Myriophyllum spicatum* L.), and didymo (*Didymosphenia geminata* [Lyngb.] M. Schmidt)—also threaten Shoshone aquatic habitats (USDA Forest Service 2009c). Non-native fish species (for example, brown trout [*Salmo trutta*] and rainbow trout [*Oncorhynchus mykiss*]) threaten native Yellowstone cutthroat trout populations by competition and hybridization (USDA Forest Service 2009c) (Table 11). The pathogen brucellosis affects elk and cattle (Cross and others 2010).

Climate Change Effects on Invasives

Globally, the effects of climate change on invasive species are expected to exacerbate the spread of some species directly by increasing suitable habitat and indirectly by increased disturbance such as fire (Dukes and Mooney 1999; Dietz and Edwards 2006). Yet some invasive species may be reduced or eliminated in the western United States (Bradley and others 2009, 2010). Bradley and others (2009) used a bioclimate model for the western United States to show that precipitation was a large factor in predicting the future range of suitable area for invasive plant species. In northwest Wyoming, the projected climate conditions by 2100 contributed to for the increased spread of yellow starthistle (*Centaurea solstitialis*), cheatgrass (*Bromus tectorum*), and spotted knapweed (*Centaurea maculosa*); however, white leafy spurge (*Euphorbia esula*) was projected to contract in southwestern Montana. Tamarisk (*Tamarix* spp.) was not projected to have a large change in distribution but had a low possibility of retreat from north-central Wyoming (Bradley and others 2009). The potential consequences to ecosystem services include reduced grazing quality and habitat function impairment and decreased aesthetic value on the landscape (Table 11).

The current expansion of aquatic invasive species throughout the United States (for example, the New Zealand mudsnail currently found on the Shoshone) is expected to continue, and future dynamics are expected to involve complex interactions for multiple factors (Rahel and Olden 2008). Warmer future temperatures are expected to increase the range of suitable habitat for temperature-tolerant invading species, while increased rainfall or flooding would increase their spread and drought would be expected to hinder their spread (U.S. EPA 2008). Warmer temperatures have been found to shorten the duration of ice cover and to increase water temperatures, thereby enhancing conditions for non-native warm water species and stressing native cold water species in Canada (Sharma and others 2007). Increased demand for water resources may lead to more construction of reservoirs in the United States that can be hotspots for invasive species (Rahel and Olden 2008). Another potential consequence to ecosystem services is an enhanced competitive ability for warm water, non-native aquatic species that could hold a competitive advantage over native cold water species (Table 11).

Fire

Paleo-Historic and Recent Fire History

Historic fire behavior since 17,000 BP in the GYE has been largely influenced by climate, with major fires tending to occur during relatively dry or hot periods (Millspaugh and others 2000; Whitlock and others 2003; Higuera and

Table 11. Summary of invasive conditions for the 20th Century, projections for the 21st Century, and potential consequences to ecosystem services.

	Current trend or condition over the 20th Century	Anticipated ecological response over 21st Century	Potential consequences to ecosystem services
Climate trend	• Temperature increase of 2 to 4 °F (1 to 2 °C) (especially in winter and spring) • Precipitation and snowpack decline	• Annual temperature increase range of 2 to 10 °F (1.1 to 5.5 °C) by 2100 • Annual precipitation 10% increase with wetter winters (+10%) and drier summers (-10%) (more uncertain)	
Invasives	• Invasive plant species include knapweed, toadflax, cheatgrass, musk thistle, and oxeye daisy • Non-native fish species compete and hybridize with native Yellowstone cutthroat trout	• Increased spread of yellow starthistle, spotted knapweed, and cheatgrass • Potential contraction of white leafy spurge in GYE • Enhanced habitat for non-native, warm water species	• Potential reduction in habitat function and grazing quality • Potential decrease in aesthetic value of landscape • Potential increased competitive advantage for non-native fish over native species

others 2010). The spatial variability of fire has been influenced by elevation, forest structure, and rugged topography (Millspaugh and others 2000; Whitlock and others 2003; Higuera and others 2010). Although insufficient data exist to precisely quantify historic fire behavior on the Shoshone, it is likely that high-elevation forests—where most of the Shoshone occurs—have experienced less frequent, larger, stand replacing fires (Turner and Romme 1994) that were most likely caused by lightning. High-elevation forests of the Shoshone may have a historical mean fire interval (MFI) ranging from 150 to 700 years for high intensity, stand replacing fires and 10 to 300 years for all fire events (Meyer and others 2006). Lower-elevation forests of the Shoshone may have been more affected than higher-elevation forest by Native American burning prior to Euro-American settlement (Barrett and Arno 1982; Schoennagel and others 2004) and post Euro-American settlement fire suppression since the late 1800s. Human influences on fire in these lower-elevation forests have likely caused lower intensity fires with MFI from 20 to 200 years, which may be outside the historic range of variability (Meyer and others 2006). Since 1971, Shoshone high-elevation forests have experienced high intensity crown fires but a lower numbers of fire starts (29 starts/247,105 acres [100,000 ha]/year) compared to lower-elevation forests (USDA Forest Service, Shoshone Fire and RIS databases 1970 to 2000) (Table 12). Almost all of these fires were in whitebark pine stands (27 of the total 29) (USDA Forest Service, Shoshone Fire and RIS databases 1970 to 2000). Lower-elevation forests of the Shoshone have experienced lower intensity fires and a higher numbers of fire starts (120 starts/247,105 acres [100,000 ha]/year) than higher elevations (USDA Forest Service, Shoshone Fire

and RIS databases 1970 to 2000) (Table 12). In the last 5 years, ~115,000 acres (46,538 ha) have burned; and in the last 10 years, ~161,500 acres (65,356 ha) have burned on the Shoshone (USDA Forest Service 2011a).

Climate Change Impacts on Fire

The majority of research focuses on fire history, and projections for future fire on the Shoshone are limited (Flannigan and others 2000; Whitlock and others 2003; Smithwick and others 2009) or inferred from historic fire behavior under given climatic conditions (Romme and Turner 1991). Certainly, increased temperatures without precipitation increases can result in drier fuels and increased fire occurrence. Whitlock and others (2003) simulated potential changes in summer soil moisture for the western United States under warmer temperatures. Their simulations suggested that the mid Twenty-First Century will exhibit drier-than-present conditions similar to those of 6000 BP—a period of high fire occurrence (Whitlock and others 2003). Generally, increased temperatures can also lead to earlier and longer fire seasons that burn more area and younger forests with decreased C storage, thereby increasing forest fragmentation (Flannigan and others 2000). Earlier snowmelt at high elevations could bring more area into a longer fire season (Miller 2006). Drier conditions are expected to cause fires to be larger and may spread more often from wilderness areas (Miller 2006). An increase in fire occurrence will also create younger stands and decrease the amount of mature forest in the GYE (Romme and Turner 1991; Whitlock and others 2003). However, a fire model projects that future warming and increased atmospheric CO_2 concentrations would increase the productivity of lodgepole pine forests in YNP, resulting in a

Table 12. Summary of fire conditions for the 20th Century, projections for the 21st Century, and potential consequences to ecosystem services.

	Current trend or condition over the 20th Century	Anticipated ecological response over 21st Century	Potential consequences to ecosystem services
Climate trend	• Temperature increase of 2 to 4 °F (1 to 2 °C) (especially in winter and spring) • Precipitation and snowpack decline	• Annual temperature increase range of 2 to 10 °F (1.1 to 5.5 °C) by 2100 • Annual precipitation 10% increase with wetter winters (+10%) and drier summers (-10%) (more uncertain)	
Fire	• More fires at lower elevations of Shoshone than at higher elevations • Higher intensity fires at higher elevations of Shoshone • Increased fire activity, especially at mid elevations of Rocky Mountains	• Earlier, longer fire seasons • More burned area • More fragmentation • Younger, more fire resistant forest species • Less C storage • Uncertain role of human interactions (ignitions and fire suppression) and bark beetle outbreaks in the future fire regime	• Increased fire occurrence may cause more post-fire areas to be affected by short-term degradation of terrestrial and aquatic habitat • Potential spatial and temporal variability and reduction of C sequestration ability

reduction of the time needed to recover C stocks to pre-fire levels (Smithwick and others 2009).

The indirect effects of future climate warming may also influence future fire regimes on the Shoshone. Increased temperature, winter precipitation, and atmospheric CO_2 concentration may enhance primary productivity of re-growth following fire in western forests (Powell and Hansen 2007), increasing fuel loads and contributing to more severe fires than present (Whitlock and others 2003). Warmer and earlier springs have been associated with an increase in large, western United States wildfire activity since the mid 1980s, especially in the mid elevations of the northern Rockies (Westerling and others 2006). Likewise, increased fires would enhance the expansion of fire adapted species, such as lodgepole pine, and create environmental conditions suitable for invasion by non-native plants (Bartlein and others 1997). Overall, fires are expected to increase in frequency and severity under future climate change, but it is uncertain what role interacting human factors, such as human caused fire ignitions and fire suppression efforts, will play. The effects of other future disturbance, such as bark beetle epidemics, are also uncertain as bark beetle outbreaks have been found to both increase and decrease fire occurrence and severity (see the "Insect and Pathogen" section) (Table 12). The potential consequence to ecosystem services from the projected changes in the fire regime may be an increase in post-fire area affected by short-term terrestrial and aquatic habitat degradation. Also, the C sequestration potential of

the landscape may be reduced and may vary spatially and temporally (Table 12).

Insects and Pathogens

Current Conditions

Native insects, such as bark beetles (*Dendroctonus* spp., including Mountain Pine beetle [*Dendroctonus pondersae*], Spruce beetle [*Dendroctonus rufipennis*], and Douglas-fir beetle [*Dendroctonus pseudotsugae*]) are endemic species of western U.S. forests and are important ecological regulators that aid in the sustained regeneration of forests (Logan and Powell 2001). Beetle population dynamics are influenced by stand conditions (Amman 1977), host availability and susceptibility (Breshears and others 2005), land management (Keane and others 2002), climate (Logan and Powell 2001), disturbance history, and predation. Epidemic outbreaks occur periodically, resulting in large tracts of dead stands (Logan and Powell 2001; Kurz and others 2008) that reduce the ability of land managers to meet short-term desired conditions and management objectives (USDA Forest Service 2009b).

The Shoshone hosts endemic bark beetles that have been at epidemic proportions within the last 10 years, resulting in substantial mortality, especially of larger diameter trees (USDA Forest Service 2009c). By 2010, the Douglas-fir beetle has caused mortality over roughly 203,000 acres (82,151 ha) of the total 373,000 acres (150,948 ha) of

Table 13. Summary of insect and pathogen Conditions for the 20th Century, projections for the 21st Century, and potential consequences to ecosystem services.

	Current trend or condition over the 20th Century	Anticipated ecological response over 21st Century	Potential consequences to ecosystem services
Climate trend	• Temperature increase of 2 to 4 °F (1 to 2 °C) (especially in winter and spring) • Precipitation and snowpack decline	• Annual temperature increase range of 2 to 10 °F (1.1 to 5.5 °C) by 2100 • Annual precipitation 10% increase with wetter winters (+10%) and drier summers (-10%) (more uncertain)	
Insects and pathogens	• Bark beetle outbreaks in lodgepole pine, ponderosa pine, five-needle pine, Douglas-fir, and spruce forests since 1996 causing moderate to high tree mortality on ~1,086,000 acres (439,438 ha) of the Shoshone's 1.4 million forested acres (566,599 ha) by 2010 • Over 100,000 acres (40,468 ha) affected by both white pine blister rust and pine beetle • The number of acres affected by bark beetles and blister rust has been increasing since 2000.	• Moderate probability of increased number of bark beetle outbreaks on Shoshone and GYE, shifting to higher elevation and northward • High temporal and spatial variability of bark beetle outbreaks • Little is known about future pathogen dynamics under climate change	• Reduced aesthetic and timber value • Potential increase in the variability and possibility of forested areas at higher elevations on the Shoshone turning into carbon sources after beetle outbreaks

Douglas-fir stands (USDA Forest Service 2011b) (Table 13). The spruce beetle has also caused mortality on about 278,000 acres (112,502 ha) of the total 348,000 acres (140,830 ha) of spruce forest. The number of Douglas-fir and spruce beetle affected acres has increased since 2009 (USDA Forest Service 2011b) (Table 13). Lodgepole pine and threatened five-needle pines (whitebark pine and bristlecone pine) are affected by the mountain pine beetle in the Rocky Mountains (Koteen 2002; Tomback and Resler 2007). Prior to 2010, mountain pine beetle activity on the Shoshone has increased and has affected 605,000 acres (244,835 ha) of lodgepole, ponderosa, and five-needle pine forests since 1996 (USDA Forest Service 2011b) (Table 13).

Over 100,000 acres (40,469 ha) of the Shoshone have been affected by both the mountain pine beetle and the white pine blister rust (USDA Forest Service 2009c) (Table 13), which can reduce tree resistance to beetle attacks (Parker and others 2006). Comandra blister rust (*Cronartium*

comandrae Pk.) and the parasitic plant dwarf mistletoe (*Arceuthobium* sp.) are widespread on the southern part of the Forest. Comandra blister rust and dwarf mistletoe serve as suppression agents that leave the hosts more vulnerable to stressors, such as drought and insect attacks (USDA Forest Service 2009a, 2009c). Blister rust and mountain pine beetle have been observed to attack whitebark pine simultaneously, creating different spatial patterns of tree mortality (Hatala and others 2009). Spatially clustered patches of mortality with infilling dominated in blister rust-infected areas at two sites just north of the Shoshone, while more spatially contiguous mountain pine beetle mortality patterns dominated a site near the northwestern border of YNP (Hatala and others 2009).

The interactions between beetles and fire are well documented in the literature (McCullough and others 1998; Logan and Powell 2001; Kulakowski and others 2003; Lynch and others 2006); however, these interactions are not well understood (Bentz 2005). Retrospective studies have shown both increases and decreases of fire intensity, extent, and severity in post-beetle outbreak areas of the Rocky Mountains. The longer-term influence of mountain pine beetle outbreaks has been found to slightly increase the severity and probability of fire occurrence and to increase fuel loads in the Rocky Mountains of northern Colorado and YNP (Turner and others 1999; Bigler and others 2005; Lynch and others 2006). However, stand structure was found to be a better predictor of fire severity (Bigler and others 2005). Simard (2010) found that for GYE lodgepole pine forests, the probability of active crown fire was decreased for 35 years after beetle outbreak, but the probability of passive crown fire increased when understory growth provided vertical continuity between the forest floor and tree crowns. A decrease in, or no impact to, fire occurrence, extent, and severity has been observed in subalpine areas of mountain pine beetle and spruce beetle outbreak areas in Colorado and the GYE (Bebi and others 2003; Kulakowski and others 2003; Kulakowski and Veblen 2007; Simard and others 2008). Surface fire intensity was predicted to increase for Douglas-fir, spruce, and pine stands with beetle outbreaks 0 to 5 years after an outbreak, but crown fire intensity was predicted to decrease 5 to 60 years after a beetle outbreak (Jenkins and others 2008). Fuel characteristics are altered over the course of the bark beetle epidemic, potentially resulting in increased or decreased fire intensity and severity (Jenkins and others 2008). Beetle outbreak occurrence may also be dependent on the availability of suitable hosts. Paleoecologic evidence shows that mountain pine beetle outbreaks occurred 8000 BP during a cooler and wetter period with low fire occurrence, when there was a prevalence of susceptible whitebark pine hosts in Idaho and Montana (Brunelle and others 2008) that likely were not exposed to blister rust.

Increased bark beetle outbreaks may also alter the C cycle in ecosystems. Kurz and others (2008) found the cumulative effects of large-scale, unprecedented beetle outbreaks to convert lodgepole pine forests to large net C sources, as opposed to the net sinks that occurred in British Columbia, Canada[3]. This could effectively negate any potential C sink enhancement effects; such has longer growing seasons, expanded range, and CO_2 and nitrogen (N) fertilization (Hansen and others 2001; Kurz and others 2008; Smithwick and others 2009).

Climate Change Effects on Insects and Pathogens

Climate change may be altering the dynamics between bark beetles and forests. Increased temperatures may be one factor that results in higher rates of insect outbreaks when suitable hosts are available (Logan and Powell 2001;

Romme and others 2006). Under a warmer climate, many forest insects will experience greater survival, reproduction, and development rates (Bentz 2005; Hicke and others 2006). Range expansions are possible as more habitat becomes suitable for host establishment (Bale and others 2002; Ryan and others 2008). Likewise, increased drought stress and warmer temperatures may cause some plant species to exhibit a decline in their capacity to resist insect attack (Ayres and Lombardero 2000). Bentz and others' (2010) modeling study projected a large increase in the probability of spruce beetle outbreaks and a moderate increase in the probability of mountain pine beetle outbreaks over the next century on the Shoshone and GYE. Future beetle outbreaks may shift northward and upward in elevation, be highly variable spatially and temporally, and result in forest ecosystem regime shifts beyond historical bounds (Bentz and others 2010). These outbreaks also leave behind dead and decaying trees that have decreased wood product value (Lowell and others 2010).

Bark beetles will likely follow the range of hosts as they track changes in climate, abandoning areas where the climate becomes too warm (Bentz 2005). Concurrently, bark beetles are capable of responding to climate changes faster than tree species (Bentz 2005). Evidence of this expansion has already occurred in British Columbia, Canada, where an increased area of mature pine stands in recent decades has resulted in unprecedented outbreaks of mountain pine beetle (Kurz and others 2008). Thus, elevated temperatures at higher altitudes could allow for mountain pine beetles to attack five-needle pines—suitable hosts that, to date, have been buffered from attack by harsh climate (Logan and Powell 2001). Carroll and others (2006) found an increase in mountain pine beetle presence in formerly unsuitable habitat in Canada that "can only be explained by changes in climate." Overall, the potential consequences to ecosystem services include reduced aesthetic and commercial timber value on the landscape and an increase in the variability and number of forested areas turning into C sources after beetle outbreaks at higher elevations on the Shoshone (Table 13).

Wildlife

Current Conditions

The Shoshone supports a variety of mammal, bird, amphibian, and invertebrates, of which 25 species of are special management interest and concern (USDA Forest Service 2009c). Some species have limited ranges, and other species such as bighorn sheep (*Ovis canadensis*), elk (*Cervus elaphus*), mule deer (*Odocoileus hemionus*), bald eagle (*Haliaeetus leucocephalus*), coyotes (*Canis latrans*), and gray wolves (*Canis lupus*) can move long distances between summer and winter ranges. The large extent of roadless and wilderness areas on the Shoshone provides crucial connected habitat for these wide ranging species. Riparian areas are also an important a source of water, forage, prey, and cover. Endangered species such as Canada lynx (*Lynx canadensis*) are rare in the GYE, and black footed ferrets (*Mustela*

---

[3] The cumulative impact of beetle outbreaks is the combined effect of beetle kill, fire, and harvesting on productivity. Carbon balance and forest productivity were modeled from 2000 to 2020 using the Carbon Budget Model of the Canadian Forest Sector (CMB-CFS3). Climate was not explicitly modeled.

Table 14. Summary of wildlife conditions for the 20th Century, projections for the 21st Century, and potential consequences to ecosystem services.

	Current trend or condition over the 20th Century	Anticipated ecological response over 21st Century	Potential consequences to ecosystem services
Climate trend	• Temperature increase of 2 to 4 °F (1 to 2 °C) (especially in winter and spring) • Precipitation and snowpack decline	• Annual temperature increase range of 2 to 10 °F (1.1 to 5.5 °C) by 2100 • Annual precipitation 10% increase with wetter winters (+10%) and drier summers (-10%) (more uncertain)	
Wildlife	• Big game, eagle, and wolf populations are stable or increasing but are spatially variable on the Shoshone. • Amphibian populations may be declining in YNP.	• Increased spatial variability, phenology changes, and population changes of wildlife associated with changes in food source locations and vegetation distribution • Higher adaptability potential by species with large habitat ranges, wider diet and environment tolerance, and higher reproductive rates (for example, birds, coyote, and grizzly bear) • Lower adaptability potential by species that are located at the margins of climate tolerance, have slow reproduction rates, or have narrow environmental tolerances (for example, amphibians, lynx, and wolverines)	• Potential high-elevation refugia for species seeking cooler habitats • Potential reduction of suitable habitat and species that are unable to adapt

nigripes) are not known to occur on the Shoshone but have been reintroduced in southern Wyoming. Populations of moose (*Alces alces*) have recently declined, which is thought to be due to drought (USDA Forest Service 2011a). Amphibian populations may also be declining in the GYE (Corn 2007; McMenamin and others 2008). Brucellosis infections of elk have been increasing (Xie 2008), although the infection's effect on elk populations is statistically undetectable (Cross and others 2010). Shoshone large-scale population trends for gray wolf, grizzly bear, bald eagle, elk, and big horn sheep have been stable or increasing over the last decade, but population trends vary at the local scale (Wyoming Game and Fish 2008; USDA Forest Service 2009c; Jimenez and others 2010) (Table 14).

Climate Change Effects on Wildlife

Globally, climate change effects on wildlife have already been noted to cause shifts in species populations, distribution, and phenology (Root and Schneider 2002; Parmesan 2006, 2007). Throughout the western hemisphere, climate change is expected to effect the largest shifts in faunal change in the coming century, with the greatest effects occurring at high elevations and high latitudes (Lawler and others 2009).

Generally, species that are range restricted (for example, those that are on mountaintops or are endemics), are located at the margins of climate tolerance, have slow reproduction rates, or have narrow environmental tolerances (for example, amphibians, lynx, and wolverines [*Gulo gulo*]) are projected to be the most sensitive to climate change and experience the largest range contractions, population reductions, and extinctions (Parmesan 2006; Ohlemuller and others 2008). Species that have larger habitat ranges (for example, elk and deer), tolerate a wider range of environment and diet (for example, coyote), and reproduce more quickly (for example, insects or birds) are expected to be less affected by climate change. For example, bird species have been expanding their range in Wyoming (Joyce and others 2008b). Also, the presence of certain species may function to buffer the effects of climate change. Modeling results for Wilmers and Getz (2005) and Wilmers and Post (2006) projected a warmer climate to reduce late winter carrion for scavenger species, such as grizzly bear, but these reductions were buffered by the presence of gray wolf within YNP increasing the availability of carrion.

Vegetation distribution changes or reductions of food sources may ultimately determine the future dynamics of wildlife populations. Although climate change effects on wildlife biodiversity have not been specifically studied on the Shoshone, GYE studies may apply. High-elevation habitat of the GYE is predicted to fragment and shrink (Romme and Turner 1991; Schrag and others 2008), and may contribute to the relocation or reduction of many mammals (for example, grizzly bear, mountain goat, pika, and lynx). For example, grizzly bear habitat in the subalpine may be linked to whitebark pine (Koteen 2002). Whitebark pine seeds are larger and more nutritious than other conifer seeds, offering grizzly bears an important food resource at higher elevations (7500 to 9000 ft or 2288 to 2745 m) (Koteen 2002). In subalpine forests of the GYE, whitebark pine is considered a keystone species that has been declining due to white pine blister rust, mountain pine beetle outbreaks, and fire suppression (Koteen 2002; Schrag and others 2008). Continued decline of whitebark pine could cause grizzly bears to shift to lower elevations where other food sources exist, potentially moving the bears closer to humans and outside of Federal protected areas (Mattson and others 1992; Schwartz and others 2010). Grizzly bears have been observed to move to lower elevations during years when whitebark pine seed crops are poor (Mattson and others 1992). Additionally, grizzly bear populations have been relatively stable within YNP but are expanding outside of the park (Schwartz and others 2006). Elk migrations have been found to be related to the severity and duration of the previous winter, and elk populations have also been expanding north outside of YNP (White and others 2010). The elk expansion could influence wolf populations to expand concurrently (White and others 2010).

Potential consequences to ecosystem services are that the Shoshone may serve as high-elevation refugia for species seeking cooler habitats, while some habitats and species may be reduced and/or redistributed, especially at lower elevations (Table 14).

Fish

Current Conditions

The Shoshone has approximately 3850 miles (6200 km) of perennial streams, of which about 1492 miles (2401 km) are occupied by Yellowstone cutthroat trout, and 395 miles (636 km) are occupied by non-hybridized Yellowstone cutthroat trout (Figure 20) (Table 15). Stream slope has been found to be a strong predictor (model accuracy of 83 percent) of the presence of Yellowstone cutthroat trout in the Absaroka Mountains on the Shoshone (Kruse and others 1999). The trout generally do not occur on slopes steeper than 10 percent, and populations linearly increase as slope decreases (Kruse and others 1999).Yellowstone cutthroat trout are native to the GYE and have been partially displaced or hybridized with the introduction of non-native trout species (DeRito and others 2010). Hybridization of Yellowstone cutthroat trout has been found to occur in the Yellowstone River due to the spatial and temporal overlap of spawning periods for Yellowstone cutthroat trout (beginning during June and July) and rainbow trout and hybrids (beginning during

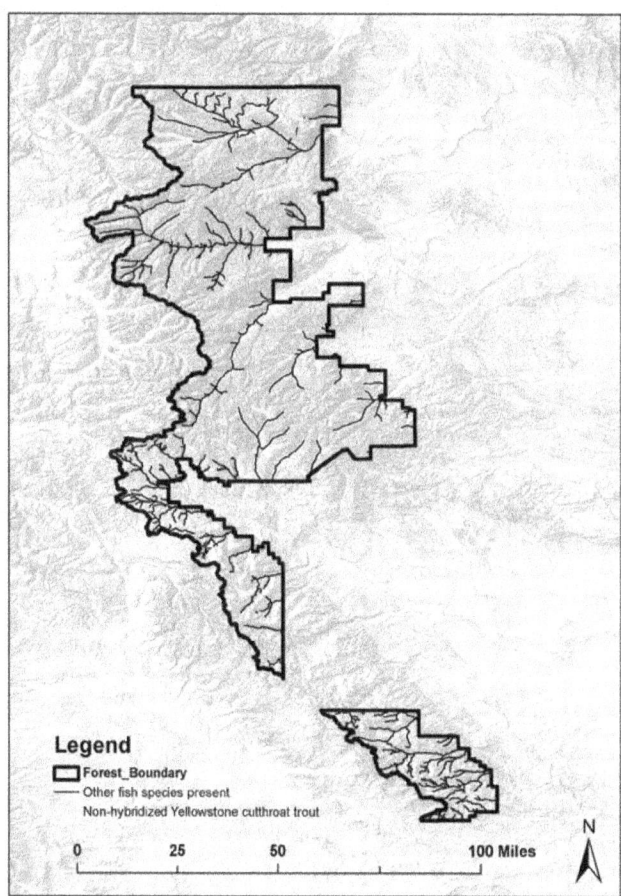

Figure 20. Distribution of non-hybridized Yellowstone cutthroat trout and other fish present (other fish can include hybridized Yellowstone cutthroat trout).

April and May) (DeRito and others 2010). The separation of the majority of spawning periods has helped preserve some of the native Yellowstone cutthroat trout populations; however, competition from other non-native species, especially at young stages, has been shown in models to eventually displace and threaten the extinction of Yellowstone cutthroat trout (Van Kirk and others 2009).

Climate Change Effects on Fish

Flows are a primary control for fish that are highly sensitive to climate change (Rieman and Isaac 2010) as salmonid habitat availability can be limited by stream flow. Low flows can reduce habitat, forcing a migration to more suitable habitat (Gregory and others (2009). Gregory and others (2009) found that Yellowstone cutthroat trout move as much as 25 miles (40 km) up or downstream prior to spawning in the East Fork Wind River. Future Wind River stream flows have been projected to be reduced overall, with further decreases in late summer and increases during peak spring runoff (Stonefeldt and others 2000). Peak flows have been projected to occur four to five weeks earlier under climate change in the western United States (Stewart and others 2004). Stream flow may become more dominated by rain instead of snow melt,

Table 15. Summary of fish conditions for the 20th Century, projections for the 21st Century, and potential consequences to ecosystem services.

	Current trend or condition over the 20th Century	Anticipated ecological response over 21st Century	Potential consequences to ecosystem services
Climate trend	• Temperature increase of 2 to 4 °F (1 to 2 °C) (especially in winter and spring) • Precipitation and snowpack decline	• Annual temperature increase range of 2 to 10 °F (1.1 to 5.5 °C) by 2100 • Annual precipitation 10% increase with wetter winters (+10%) and drier summers (-10%) (more uncertain)	
Fish	• The Shoshone has ~3850 miles (6196 km) of perennial streams • Yellowstone cutthroat trout (including hybridized) and other fish species occupy ~1492 stream miles (2401 km), largely in the central and northern Shoshone • Non-hybridized Yellowstone cutthroat trout occupy about 361 stream miles (581 km). • Cold temperature may be limiting fish habitat.	• Reduced summer stream flow, increased spring runoff, and earlier peak runoffs may further limit salmonid habitat and could hinder spawning activity. • Higher temperatures may hinder or reduce salmonid habitat, especially at lower elevations. • Higher-elevation salmonid habitat may improve as stream temperatures increase; however, higher numbers of smaller tributaries and more fragmented habitat at higher elevations. • Warmer temperatures may shift the competitive advantage to non-native and larger trout.	• Potential shifts or reductions in suitable salmonid habitat and associated fish species • Potential reduction or loss of recreational opportunities for fishing native cold water species with the reduction in habitat quality and area • Potential decrease in recreational fishing opportunities • Potential high-elevation refugia for fish seeking cooler habitats

especially at lower elevation, with earlier peak flows and lower summer flows (San Francisco basin, Knowles and Cayan 2004; Washington, Elsner and others 2010). Lower summer flows may limit salmonid habitat availability, and peak flows or flooding can hinder spawning activity (Gregory and others 2009).

In addition to stream flow, stream temperature is another control that can limit salmonid habitat. Stream temperatures have been found to have a strong relationship with air temperatures (Webb and Noblis 2007; Kaushal and others 2010). Keleher and Rahel (1996) found the distribution of Rocky Mountain salmonids to be limited by temperature—salmonids were restricted to areas where average July air temperatures do not exceed 72 °F (22 °C).

Cold-adapted fish species ranges are projected to generally shift upward in elevation due to downstream temperature increases, and to become increasingly fragmented and disjointed from larger streams that naturally hold source populations (Keleher and Rahel 1996). Future air temperature increases for the high-elevation areas of the Shoshone are predicted to range from 6 to 18 °F (3.3 to 10 °C) by 2100. In the State of Wyoming, using an air temperature increase projection of 6

°F (3.3 °C), salmonid habitat could be reduced ~38 percent (Keleher and Rahel 1996). An air temperature increase of 9 °F (5 °C) could result in approximately a 68 percent reduction of the current area suitable for salmonids (Keleher and Rahel 1996). However, increased temperatures may improve habitat for native cutthroat trout at higher elevations, and isolated headwater streams may provide protection from non-native invasive trout (Cook and others 2010). But the smaller tributaries and lower populations supported at these higher elevations have been projected to experience decreased genetic variability and probability of native trout survival (Cook and others 2010).

Stream temperature increases may also indirectly affect cutthroat trout populations by altering inter-species competition. Jenkins and Keeley's (2010) bioenergetic modeling study in the Yellowstone River found that increasing temperatures can extend the growing season, benefiting larger fish if suitable habitat exists; but higher temperatures consistently had a negative effect on smaller sizes of fish with higher metabolisms. (Bioenergetic models estimate the net energy intake rates to estimate the profitability of stream habitat by calculating the energetic costs and benefits of foraging locations.)

Non-native brook trout have been shown to behavioral-ly dominate cutthroat trout and gather more food at higher temperatures, further tipping the competitive balance to non-native trout (Hauer and others 1997). Thus, increased water temperature reduces salmonid habitat (especially at lower elevations), improves stream habitat for native trout at higher elevations where there is a higher number of smaller tributaries and more fragmented habitat, and can shift the competitive advantage to non-native and larger trout (Table 15).

Glacial loss, reduced stream flow (especially in late summer), and increased water temperatures have been found to negatively affect aquatic organisms in the Rocky Mountains (Hauer and others 1997). Fish populations in the streams of the Rocky Mountains are dominated by salmonids, whose habitat could be highly susceptible to climate warming (Hauer and others 1997). Potential consequences to ecosystem services include shifted or reduced salmonid habitat and associated species, and reduced recreational fishing opportunities for native cold water fish if salmonid habitat is reduced or degraded. Also, the Shoshone may serve as a high-elevation refugium for salmonid populations (Table 15).

Biochemical Cycling

Current Conditions

Here, we focus on C and N cycling, because the former helps to offset atmospheric CO_2 from fossil fuel emissions (MEA 2005; Ryan and others 2008), and the latter can limit forest productivity and C sequestration potential (Fahey and others 1985; Luo and others 2004; Smithwick and others 2009). Several interacting factors can influence C and N-cycling in forests directly or indirectly. The factors that are likely to affect the Shoshone include: increased nitrogen oxide (NO_x) emissions in surrounding areas; fire and insect disturbance that alter forest structure and soil properties; and changes in forest productivity from climate (for example, precipitation and temperature) or atmospheric CO_2 increase and N deposition. Forests on the Shoshone currently sequesters roughly 22 to 33 million tons (20 to 30 million metric tons) of C and are thought to be N limited (Fahey and others 1985; Turner and others 2007; Romme and others 2009), although N deposition may be occurring from upwind agricultural and oil and gas development (USDA Forest Service 2009c) (Table 16). Future activities could lead to more NO_x emissions (Story and others 2005). Glacial melt water has recently had increased N concentrations in high-elevation streams in the Colorado Front Range (Baron and others 2009). The increase in N may not only be caused by increased atmospheric N deposition, but also may be the result of flushing microbially active, N enriched sediment from glacial melt water that may already be N enriched (Baron and others 2009).

Climate Change Effects on Biochemical Cycling

Climate change will likely have both direct (increased productivity) and indirect (shifted disturbance regimes) effects on biochemical cycling on the Shoshone. Several interacting factors under climate change can influence C cycling: (1) disturbance such as fire, insect outbreaks, windthrow, and ice storms, (2) increased productivity of forests due to higher temperatures and precipitation in areas where temperature or precipitation limits growth, (3) higher atmospheric CO_2 and

Table 16. Summary of biochemical cycling conditions for the 20th Century, projections for the 21st Century, and potential consequences to ecosystem services.

	Current trend or condition over the 20th Century	Anticipated ecological response over 21st Century	Potential consequences to ecosystem services
Climate trend	• Temperature increase of 2 to 4 °F (1 to 2 °C) (especially in winter and spring) • Precipitation and snowpack decline	• Annual temperature increase range of 2 to 10 °F (1.1 to 5.5 °C) by 2100 • Annual precipitation 10% increase with wetter winters (+10%) and drier summers (-10%) (more uncertain)	
Biochemical cycling	• C storage is roughly 22 to 33 million tons (20 to 30 million metric tons) on the Shoshone. • The Shoshone forests are N limited.	• Increased fire or insect disturbance could result in forests shifting C balance. • N availability may be increased with warmer temperatures and increased decomposition rates, thereby increasing productivity, but future frequent fire activity (<95-year return) may cause N loss.	• Potential for less C sequestration with younger forests • Potential shift to C source instead of C sink in areas of disturbance • Potential increase in forest productivity from higher N. This may be offset by increased fire frequency.

increased N deposition, and (4) decreased forest productivity from drought or nutrient limitation. C storage generally decreases after a disturbance and then increases as trees grow larger (Kashian and others 2006). More frequent fires or insect outbreaks could result in younger stands that assimilate less C than intermediate and old-growth stands (Romme and Turner 1991; Kashian and others 2006). Increased forest productivity associated with elevated atmospheric CO_2 could directly result in increased C uptake from the atmosphere (Powell and Hansen 2007). Faster-than-present post-fire productivity responses to fire have been simulated in lodgepole pine forests at YNP (Smithwick and others 2009). Also, at higher elevations where trees grow near the temperature limit, increased temperature with sufficient precipitation may directly result in greater productivity (Ryan and others 2008). Forest productivity and C sequestration potential could increase from higher atmospheric CO_2 concentrations in young, nutrient rich, non-water limited forests (FACE experiment by Norby and others 2005); however, the evidence is not consistent (Ryan and others 2008) as higher productivity may be limited by water or N availability (Luo 2004), and transient responses have been shown in older trees and different species (Korner and others 2005). Increased fire or insect outbreak activity has the capacity to offset any C gains from climate induced increases in temperature, precipitation, atmospheric CO_2 or N fertilization (Kashian and others 2006; Kurz and others 2008). However, Kashian and others (2006) suggested that the fire return interval would have to decrease to 80 years before any noticeable shift in the total C balance of the GYE would occur.

The coniferous N limited forests on the Shoshone (Fahey and others 1985; Turner and others 2007; Romme and others 2009) could experience an increase in productivity if an increase in N availability occurs. Warmer temperatures and increased precipitation could accelerate decomposition rates and directly increase N turnover. Smithwick and others (2005) simulated N dynamics for lodgepole pine under future climate scenarios (using the Canadian Climate Center and Hadley GCMs) and found that net N mineralization did not increase, but available N did increase as a function of precipitation and increased rates of decomposition. Thus, under future climate, more N may be readily available for plant uptake due to increased rates of decomposition, which would increase productivity. However, climate change may influence N-cycling in the Shoshone by altering the fire regime (Romme and Turner 1991; Turner and others 2007; Romme and others 2009; Smithwick and others 2009). There is an increased potential for N losses via nitrate leaching with more frequent fires (Hansen 2007; Turner and others 2007). Turner and others (2007) found that immobilization rates of ammonium increased after the Yellowstone fires, prohibiting nitrate buildup. However, a longer-term simulation study by Smithwick and others (2009) indicated that fire return intervals would have to decrease to about 95 years to affect long-term N storage in lodgepole pine ecosystems. Overall, a possible consequence to ecosystem services is decreased C sequestration potential, with areas of disturbance becoming C sources as opposed to C sinks. Also, forests on the Shoshone may become more productive if N is increased; however, increased disturbance may offset these productivity gains (Table 16).

Economies

Current Conditions

Recreation and tourism are major economic activities in the GYE and Shoshone (Power 1991; Rasker and Hansen 2000; USDA Forest Service 2009c). The tourism and recreation economy in the three-county area of the Shoshone was more than $350 million in 2006 (Table 17). During 2002 and 2003, the five top recreation activities on the Shoshone were: (1) viewing natural features (60 percent), (2) viewing wildlife (55 percent), (3) relaxing (48 percent), (4) hiking/walking (38 percent), and (5) driving for pleasure (33 percent), followed by picnicking (16 percent), fishing (14 percent), nature study (13 percent), visiting historical sites (10 percent), and hunting (10 percent) (Taylor and others 2008). (Individuals surveyed may have indicated more than one activity.)

Agriculture is also an important economic activity that grossed about $170 million in the three-county area in 2005 (USDA Forest Service 2009c). Snowmelt is the major source of water for agriculture in the western United States (Baron and others 2000b), and it is also used for hydropower energy generation at the Buffalo Bill (40 to 110 GWt/year) and Shoshone dams (15 to 23 GWt/year) (USBR 2007a, 2007b) (Table 17).

Domestic livestock grazing is an important activity on the Shoshone that supported over 62,500 animal unit months in 2007, resulting in $2.6 million of production, $5.4 million of total economic activity, $1.7 million in labor earnings, and 52 jobs in the region's economy (Taylor and others 2008) (Table 17).

Climate Change Effects on the Economies

Few specific studies have been focused on the economy of the area surrounding the Shoshone. We draw from economic studies in the United States and GYE and extend the potential ecological impacts to the economic sectors surrounding the Shoshone.

Nature based recreation and tourism are lucrative economic activities in Montana that are increasing and are expected to continue to increase as the population grows (Swanson 2008). Climate change may directly (weather related) and indirectly (resource related) affect recreation (Richardson and Loomis 2004), with variable effects depending on the individual preference of the recreator and the magnitude of climate change. For example, if climate change caused less water to be available in reservoirs and streams, fewer recreational opportunities would exist though the demand would be increasing. On the other hand, increased flooding under climate change may pose new risks to recreators using riparian areas.

Table 17. Summary of economic conditions for the 20th Century, projections for the 21st Century, and potential consequences to ecosystem services.

	Current trend or condition over the 20th Century	Anticipated ecological response over 21st Century	Potential consequences to ecosystem services
Climate trend	• Temperature increase of 2 to 4°F (1 to 2 °C) (especially in winter and spring) • Precipitation and snowpack decline	• Annual temperature increase range of 2 to 10 °F (1.1 to 5.5 °C) by 2100 • Annual precipitation +10% increase with wetter winters (+10%) and drier summers (-10%) (more uncertain)	
Economies	• $350 million in tourist activity • $170 million in agricultural activity • $5.4 million in livestock grazing total economic activity • Hydropower generation (40 to 100 GWt/year at Buffalo Bill Dam and 15 to 23 GWt/year at Shoshone Dam)	• Longer tourist seasons • Reduced and unreliable water resources for agriculture and hydropower	• Potential increase in summer recreation and tourism opportunities but decreased winter recreation opportunities • Potential decrease in agricultural production and hydropower generation with reduced water supply • Potential short-term reduction of grazing area by conifer encroachment, followed by eventual increase in grazing area as future climate causes grasslands to expand

Potential consequences to ecosystem services are increased summer recreation and tourism activity and fewer winter recreation opportunities (Table 17). An analysis of climate change effects on visitation in Rocky Mountain National Park indicated the net effect would be slightly positive for tourism (Richardson and Loomis 2004). Richardson and Loomis' (2004) survey respondents said their visitation behavior would change in response to hypothetical climate scenarios, a majority of which stated that driving Trail Ridge Road is a major attraction to the park. Recent warmer temperatures have allowed Trail Ridge Road to be open longer, thus the potential for increased tourism. Visitors to the Shoshone in 2003 cited viewing natural features, viewing wildlife, and driving for pleasure as their main recreational activities (Taylor and others 2008), which could portend similar results to those from the Rocky Mountain National Park study. Warmer temperatures, earlier springs, and longer summers are expected to increase the demand for outdoor recreation activities that could shift to higher latitudes and altitudes in North America (Morris and Walls 2009). However, climate change may have a negative impact on winter recreation activities such as alpine skiing (Joyce and others 2001). Loomis and Crespi (1999) estimated that a 4.5 °F (2.5 °C) temperature increase and a 7 percent precipitation increase could reduce downhill and cross country skiing by 52 percent in the United States. However, reductions in these winter recreation activities and associated economic losses were projected to be offset by an increase in reservoir, beach, golf, and stream recreational activities (Loomis and Crespi 1999). Fishing and hunting activities, though not claiming the highest percentage of visits on the Shoshone (10 and 14 percent, respectively; Taylor and others 2008) are increasing in neighboring Montana (Swanson 2008).

Climate change could reduce Shoshone water supplies for hydropower generation and agriculturalists and urban areas to the east (Table 17). Water sources could become unreliable during summer months if snowmelt shifted earlier in the season (Stonefelt and others 2000; Gray and McCabe 2010), potentially causing water shortages during critical summer months (Christensen and others 2004) and leaving less water available during summer months in the western United States (Adams and Peck 2009). Model simulations at the U.S. farm level indicated decreased profits with more frequent drought conditions (Adams and Peck 2009). Adams and Peck's (2009) simulation also projected that planters were better able to adapt to more frequent but less severe drought than they were to less frequent but more severe drought, both of which are projected to occur under climate change. Losses could be mitigated by not planting low value crops, not planting on low value land, or not planting crops that require water during critical late summer months (Adams and Peck 2009). Currently, drought is estimated to cost $6 to $8 billion annually in the United States due to crop failure, municipal water shortages, wildfires, fish and wildlife mortality, and reduced hydropower generation. Mitigation planning is required to reduce the economic cost of drought (Adams and Peck 2009).

The expansion of forest into grass and shrublands that has been observed on the Shoshone (USDA Forest Service 2009c) could continue to contract suitable habitat for grazing in the short term. Some studies have noted a decrease in forage for native ungulates under future climate change (Romme and Turner 1991), which in the short term, may also imply a reduction in domestic grazing opportunities that utilize similar habitat. However, many factors (for example, sufficient precipitation and increased tree water use efficiency from increased CO_2) must coalesce to create this effect (Romme and Turner 1991). A potential consequence to ecosystem services may be the eventual expansion of grasslands and reduction of sagebrush (Schlaepfer and others 2011) and conifers (Bachelet and others 2003) that may eventually increase the area available for grazing (Table 17).

Land Use

Current Conditions

The area surrounding the Shoshone includes lands managed by the private sector, Wind River Indian Reservation, other National Forests, the Bureau of Land Management, the State of Wyoming, National Park Service, and The Nature Conservancy (Figure 21). Among the fastest growing counties in the United States (Figure 22; United States Census 2010) are those surrounding Yellowstone National Park, directly west of the Shoshone (Rasker and Hansen 2000) (Table 18). Expansion of urban areas, commercial development, and industrial development are increasing across the GYE as populations grow, and this trend is projected to continue (Gude and others 2006; Hansen 2006). Protected areas, such as designated wilderness in the Shoshone, do not function in isolation and are, in fact, parts of larger ecosystems that comprise unprotected segments vulnerable to land use change (Hansen and DeFries 2007). While the core land use of wilderness areas within the Shoshone (as protected areas)

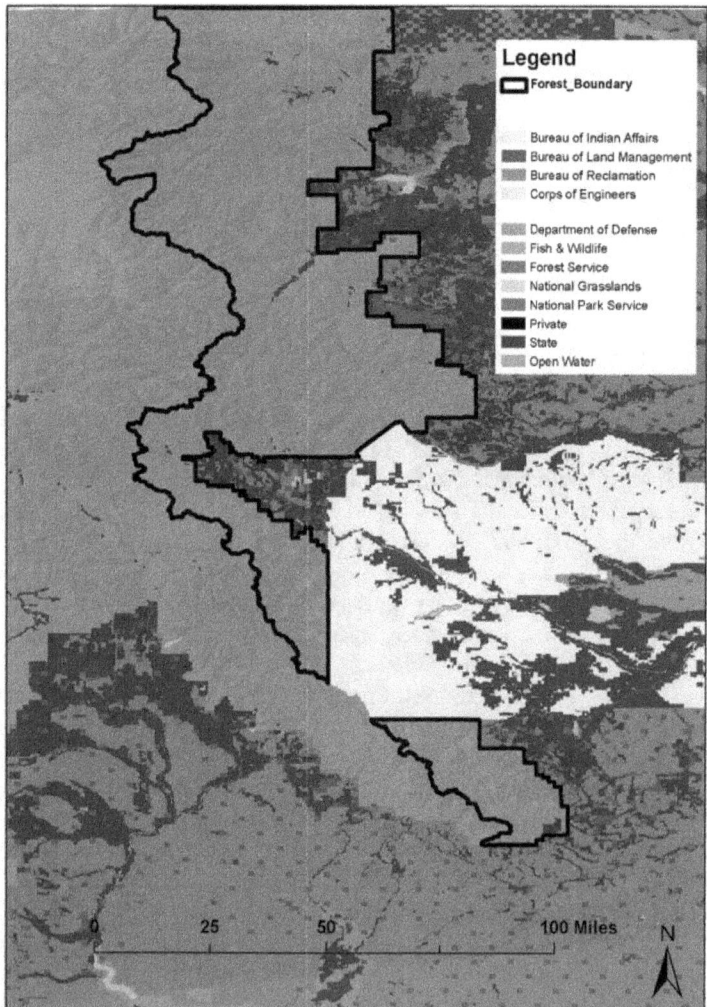

Figure 21. Wyoming land ownership.

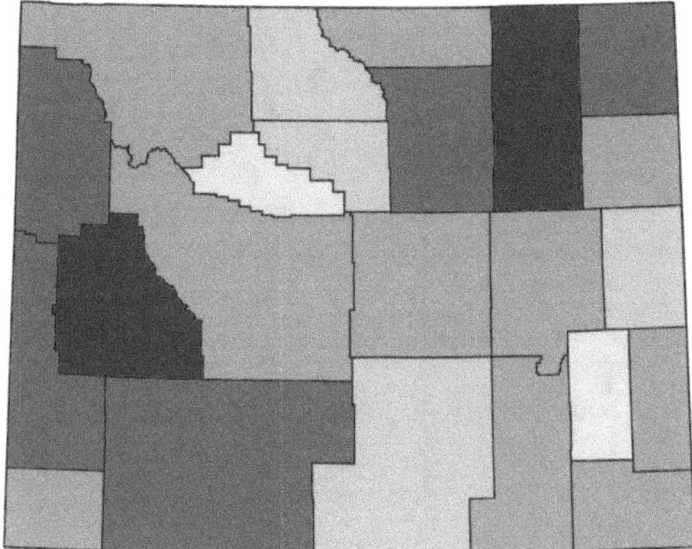

Wyoming – 2010 Census Results
State Population: 563,626

Population change by county:

| Loss | 0-5% | 5-15% | 15-25% | 25% + |

Figure 22. Wyoming population change by county, 2000-2010. Source: U.S. Census 2010.

may not change, the surrounding land uses in the GYE likely will change in the future (Gude and others 2006). Private lands comprise about 25 percent of the GYE area, mostly along the low lying riparian corridors, and are primarily used for agricultural production (Gosnell and others 2006). In the GYE, these lands are experiencing a transition in ownership from traditional ranchers to more amenity or investment owners that may manage their properties with more explicit conservation goals like enhancing and protecting wildlife habitat and aesthetic value (Gosnell and others 2006). In Montana, although there has been population growth and an increase in development of some rural lands, the loss of agricultural land on a regional scale has been minimal (Johnson 2008). Rural home sites have mostly been in shrublands or forested areas at higher elevations, while agricultural lands are mostly in riparian bottomlands and are projected to remain in agricultural production even though there is a shift in the use of these lands to more amenity purposes (Johnson 2008).

Land use change bordering protected areas can have multiple effects on ecosystem function (Hansen and others 2002). It can effectively shrink the size of the ecosystem; alter biogeochemical flows; disrupt source-sink dynamics by fragmenting corridors and/or eliminating important habitats; and create negative edge effects (Hansen and DeFries 2007). The growth rates of available housing within 31 miles (50 km) of wilderness areas in northwest Wyoming have increased over 200 percent since 1940, and in some cases, over

400 percent (Radeloff and others 2010). When coupled with a changing climate, these land use effects can be compounded (Dale 1997).

Land use change directly influences climate (for example, changes in albedo [a measure of how much a surface reflects sunlight, which determines its visual brightness and affects the temperature] and C-cycling) and can also intensify climate change related effects on the ecosystem (Dale 1997). Several studies show increased human presence and influence bordering the GYE (Rasker and Hansen 2000; Hansen and others 2002; Parmenter and others 2003; Story and others 2005; Gude and others 2006, 2007; Hansen and DeFries 2007). The type, location, and rate of land use change will likely interact with climate change in differing ways, as will policy decisions made by future stakeholders.

Exurban development is not the only new and increasing human pressure on the Shoshone. Oil and gas development in the Green River Basin, directly upwind of the Wind River Range, is also rapidly expanding (Story and others 2005). As noted by Story and others (2005), increased emissions are inextricably linked to energy development, and of greatest concern are NO_x emissions. In fact, NO_x emissions near Pinedale, Wyoming, have already reached levels six to eight times greater than originally proposed by energy projects (Story and others 2005) (Table 18). The Shoshone is currently experiencing increases in nitrate storage at the inlets of lakes, most likely from the upwind agricultural and oil and gas development (USDA Forest Service 2009c) (Table 18).

Table 18. Summary of land use conditions for the 20th Century, projections for the 21st Century, and potential consequences to ecosystem services.

	Current trend or condition over the 20th Century	Anticipated ecological response over 21st Century	Potential consequences to ecosystem services
Climate trend	• Temperature increase of 2 to 4°F (1 to 2 °C) (especially in winter and spring) • Precipitation and snowpack decline	• Annual temperature increase range of 2 to 10 °F (1.1 to 5.5 °C) by 2100 • Annual precipitation +10% increase with wetter winters (+10%) and drier summers (-10%) (more uncertain)	
Land use	• Population increase, especially west of the Shoshone • Increased NO_x emissions	• Increased urbanization bordering Federal lands in the GYE • Potential increase of NO_x emissions	• Increased landscape fragmentation and potential wildlife habitat degradation in the GYE • Increased demand for recreation, hunting, and fishing opportunities with fewer opportunities • N deposition increases potential for aquatic system acidification

Climate Change Effects on Land Use

Gude and others (2007) estimated exurban growth in the GYE by 2020 to be at least 28 percent under a low growth scenario and as high as 234 percent under a "boom" scenario. Most of the private lands available for this growth in the GYE are low-elevation, fertile valleys, which are important habitats for large animals during parts of the year and are considered "hot spots for avian biodiversity" (Gude and others 2007). Pressure on public lands and wilderness area on the Shoshone and GYE is currently moderate but is projected to increase to moderately heavy by 2020 due to non-agricultural economic development (Cordell and Overdevest 2001). Grizzly bear mortality has recently decreased in areas with secure habitat (such as Federal lands) and higher elevation, but it has increased when the density of roads, homes, developed sites, and ungulate hunting have increased in the GYE (Schwartz and others 2010). The potential consequences to ecosystem services include increased fragmentation and habitat degradation with more demand for recreational opportunities in the GYE if population growth continues (Table 18).

Along with low-elevation settlements, more development is occurring at the wild land interface directly bordering Federal lands in the GYE (Gude and others 2006; Radeloff and others 2010). Gude and others (2006) suggested that wildlife management and fire policies will certainly be influenced by these new stake-holders. Although it is likely that a greater human presence will result in greater fire suppression efforts, warmer climate has been historically linked to fire increase, even with fire suppression (Flannigan and others 2000), and more fire activity is predicted in the future

in the western United States (Whitlock and others 2003; Westerling and others 2006). The future net effect of land use and climate on fire frequency, severity, and magnitude on the Shoshone is uncertain and depends on future policy as well as climatic conditions. Nonetheless, the uncertain future of the Shoshone fire regime may alter almost every aspect of ecosystem functioning (such as C and N cycling, mountain pine beetle influence, and hydrology) and highlights the important role that land use change will play.

In the past, atmospheric N deposition on the Shoshone has been negligible but has recently been increasing from upwind agricultural and oil and gas development (Turner and others 2007; USDA Forest Service 2009c). N deposition may continue to increase with warmer temperatures, potential increases in winter precipitation due to climate change, and increased NO_x emissions due to land use change. Since the Shoshone is generally a N limited system, the projected increase could have dramatic effects on biogeochemical cycling. Smithwick and others' (2009) simulations of a lodgepole pine forest in the YNP included increased atmospheric N deposition, which was shown to bolster the direct effects of a warmer climate on forest productivity, and which could possibly enhance any potential C sink effect (Vitousek and others 1997). However, increased N deposition in aquatic systems leads to acidification and, if sufficient phosphorous exists, eutrophication[4] (Vitousek and others 1997;

---

[4] Eutrophication is a process that occurs in a body of water where dissolved oxygen is depleted by the stimulation of aquatic plant life from an enrichment of dissolved nutrients (phosphates).

Baron and others 2000b). Thus, the pristine alpine lakes of the Shoshone, and the fish populations they sustain, could be more vulnerable to eutrophication (Table 18).

Landscape fragmentation poses a great threat to biodiversity in the GYE and the Shoshone (Gude and others 2007; Radeloff and others 2010). As previously discussed, human development will directly displace some important habitat. Just as important are the isolation of remaining habitat and the disruption of species' movement. Land use change will inevitably produce barriers to traditional seasonal migrations of large animals (Gude and others 2007) and to new migrations as species track shifts in climate (Hansen and others 2001).

Migration corridors will become even more important as the landscape becomes fragmented and habitats become increasingly isolated. Gude and others (2007) found simulations of future exurban growth (by 2020) occurred disproportionately on potential mammal migration corridors. On a large scale, the genetic diversity of grizzly bears in the GYE is the lowest in continental North America (Miller and Waits 2003), owing mostly to the relative isolation of the population. Although grizzly bears have been increasing in numbers and expanding their range, natural immigration between the GYE and the Northern Continental Divide System (NCDS) in northwest Montana has not been found to occur (Haroldson and others 2010). As a result, the reduced gene flow among these isolated populations is a concern for the long-term genetic health of the grizzly bear (Haroldson and others 2010). Increased human development in linkage zones between the GYE and NCDS may decrease the likelihood of natural immigration of the grizzly bear (Haroldson and others 2010).

Knowledge and Data Gaps

In this synthesis, we have drawn on general literature when no information was available specific to the Shoshone. Many studies synthesized here focused on larger areas, such as the western United States or GYE, and study sites outside of the Shoshone, especially at YNP (for example, paleo and fire studies). Therefore, local conditions, elevation and topographic effects, and variability and extremes of climate effects may not be specifically representative of processes acting in Shoshone ecosystems.

There is a paucity of climatic, ecologic, and hydrologic data, as well as fine-scale modeling projections that capture topographic and elevation gradients that affect Shoshone climate and ecosystem processes, especially at high elevations. This lack of information produces knowledge gaps about the spatial and temporal variability of climate and affected ecosystem processes, disturbance regimes, hydrology, and human impacts.

Climate and vegetation information is sparse, especially at higher elevations. No long-term climate stations with records greater than 50 years exist above 7866 ft (2400 m) elevation in the GYE, and no climate stations with records longer than 30 years exist above 8160 ft (2490 m) within in the Shoshone. Two longer-term climate stations (early 1900s), and nine climate stations with shorter or incomplete records are on or near the Shoshone. Additionally, COOP, SNOTEL, and RAWS sites on or near the Shoshone have a limited distribution, which may or may not contribute to uncertainty in PRISM climate estimates (Figures 4, 5, and 6) at high elevations. Additionally, information is limited on current Shoshone vegetation, especially endemics and plant communities at high elevation and tree lines. Vegetation modeling for the Shoshone has been done at a 0.6-mile (1-km) scale, which may or may not capture topographic variability effects. Few studies of climate change effects on vegetation or other ecosystem functions in the GYE or the Shoshone have used the most recent GCM climate change projections from the Fourth Assessment of the IPCC (IPCC 2007b).

Specific hydrologic data and future model projects for the Shoshone are limited. Currently, there are no active gages continuously measuring stream flow on the Shoshone, and the historic gage records on or near the Shoshone (upstream of diversions) have temporal and spatial gaps. The specific magnitudes of projected variability of water quantity, timing of runoff, and evapotranspiration are not specifically known for the Shoshone. The effect of insect outbreaks on Shoshone hydrology has not been examined. Additionally, no specific published information has been found about climate effect on groundwater or water quality in the Shoshone.

Disturbance of existing ecosystems, such as insect outbreaks, fire, invasives, and their interactions with climate change have not been well studied on the Shoshone. Fire studies are more focused on YNP and the historic fire regimes on the east side of the GYE where the Shoshone lies are not well defined. Information is lacking about how human impacts, such as recreational use and management activities, on Shoshone ecosystems may affect and interact with climate change.

Although knowledge gaps exist and new information may be available in the future, we found that several resources and processes on the Shoshone may be vulnerable to climate change. The previously described gaps lead to uncertainties about how complex environmental factors interact (for example, topography-precipitation, or higher temperatures-more drought-more fire-more invasive species). While it is challenging to precisely project ecosystem responses to climate change at the local level on the Shoshone, the published records of observed trends along with well-supported hypotheses and model projections provide indications of Shoshone ecosystem vulnerabilities and responses to climate change.

Conclusion and Summary

The Shoshone has undergone and adapted to large changes in climate that have spanned thousands of years. Twentieth Century warming of 1.8 to 3.6 °F (1 to 2 °C) is expected to continue and accelerate in the next century. The expected changes in climate leave many questions as to how these ecosystems will adapt. Shoshone ecosystems are dynamic and unique components of the GYE whose higher elevations, cooler temperatures, and drier precipitation regime causes ecosystems to function differently than surrounding areas, such as YNP. Micro-climate conditions in the high elevations of the Shoshone have, and will likely continue to provide refugia for unique and sometimes rare ecologic components. These high elevations and environmental variability will likely offer opportunities for climate adaptation for some resources or species, while others may be vulnerable to undesirable effects from climate change.

In this synthesis, we identified several vulnerable and very responsive resources and processes on the Shoshone. Water resources are particularly vulnerable as warmer temperatures are projected to reduce snowpacks, increase evaporation, lengthen summer seasons, and start spring run-off earlier. Warmer temperatures are likely to lead to reduced stream flows, which are critical to habitat and reservoir storage for agricultural and human uses. However, the potential effects of warmer temperatures may be mitigated or exacerbated by future changes in precipitation, which are more uncertain. Annual precipitation has recently increased at the scale of the GYE but has decreased at finer scales around the Shoshone. Winter precipitation is projected to increase 10 percent in the GYE and may help offset evaporative losses from higher temperatures and longer summers, but projected temperatures may negate any gains in precipitation. Summer precipitation trends remain uncertain, and future reductions (as projected for the Pacific Northwest)

would intensify water shortages at a critical time. Shoshone glaciers are highly vulnerable to climate change, and are projected to disappear early to mid-century, reducing summer flow to glacial fed streams, increasing sediment and stream temperatures. Shoshone landscapes may be more vulnerable to increased fire occurrence, magnitude, and severity as warmer temperatures cause drier conditions and longer fire seasons. Shoshone habitats and wildlife that are particularly vulnerable to climate change are alpine ecosystems, wetlands, and species that are stressed, with lower adaptive ability to higher temperatures, or existing at the edge of an environmental tolerance (for example, cold water salmonid Yellowstone cutthroat trout, lynx, pika, aspen, and whitebark pine). The genetic adaptive capacity of these and other species on the Shoshone remains an area of limited information. Grass and sagebrush on the Shoshone may continue to be vulnerable to conifer encroachment in the short term until increased temperatures and moisture limitations inhibit conifer establishment, especially at lower elevations. Hosts of insect infestations are likely to remain vulnerable to future outbreaks under warmer temperatures. Shoshone terrestrial and aquatic habitats are expected to remain vulnerable to the spread of some invasive species. Local economic sectors such as agriculture may be vulnerable to the effects of reduced water supply. Warmer temperatures and longer summers could increase summer tourism but could hinder winter tourism activities. Human activities will likely have a large influence on how Shoshone ecosystems respond in the future, especially regarding fire (fire suppression), N cycling (increase from oil and gas development), and land use (increasing fragmentation).

The interaction of Shoshone ecosystem processes with future climate change could produce unforeseeable or undesirable ecosystem changes, highlighting the need to identify potential resource vulnerabilities, and use this information to help develop adaptation strategies.

Literature Cited

Adams, R. and Peck, D. 2009. Effects of climate change on drought frequency: potential impacts and mitigation opportunities. Managing water resources in a time of global change: mountains, valleys and flood plains. A. Garrido and A. Dinar. New York, Routledge: 117-130.

Aitkin, S. 2008. Adaptation, migration or extirpation: climate change outcomes for tree populatioins. Evolutionary Applications 1(1):95-111.

Amman, G. 1977. The role of the mountain pine beetle in lodgepole pine ecosystems: impact on succession. The role of arthropods in forest ecosystems. W. J. Mattson. New York, Springer-Verlag: 3-18.

Arnell, N. 1998. Climate change and water resources in Britain. Climatic Change 39:83-110.

Ashcroft, M. 2010. Identifying refugia from climate change. Journal of Biogeography 37:1407-1413.

Ashton, I. 2010. Observed and projected ecological response to climate change in the Rocky Mountains and Upper Columbia Basin: a synthesis of current scientific literature. Natural Resource Report NPS/ROMN/ NRR—2010/220. National Park Service, Fort Collins, Colorado.

Ayres, M. and Lombardero, M. 2000. Assessing the consequences of global change for forest disturbance from herbivores and pathogens. The Science of the Total Environment 262(3):263-286.

Bachelet, D.; Neilson, R.; Lenihan, J. [and others]. 2001. Climate change effects on vegetation distribution and carbon budget in the United States. Ecosystems 4(3):164-185.

Bachelet, D.; Neilson, R.; Hickler, T. [and others]. 2003. Simulating past and future dynamics of natural ecosystems in the United States. Global Biogeochemical Cycles 17(2):1-20.

Baker, R. 1970. Pollen sequence from late quaternary sediments in Yellowstone-Park. Science 168(3938):1449-1450.

Bale, J.; Masters, G.; Hodkinson, I. [and others]. 2002. Herbivory in global climate change research: direct effects of rising temperature on insect herbivores. Global Change Biology 8(1):1-16.

Balling, R.C.; Meyer, G.; Wells, S. 1992. Climate change in Yellowstone-National-Park—is the drought-related risk of wildfires increasing? Climatic Change 22(1):35-45.

Barnett, T.; Adams, J.; Lettenmaier, D. 2005. Potential impacts of climate warming on water availability in snow dominated regions. Science 438:303-309.

Barnett, T. and Pierce, D. 2009. Sustainable water deliveries from the Colorado River in a changing climate. Proceedings of the National Academy of Sciences 106(18): 7334-7338.

Baron, J.; Rueth, H.; Wolfe A. [and others]. 2000a. Ecosystem responses to nitrogen deposition in the Colorado Front Range. Ecosystems 3(4):352-368.

Baron, J.; Hartman, M.; Band, L. [and others]. 2000b. Sensitivity of a high-elevation Rocky Mountain watershed to altered climate and CO_2. Water Resources Research 36(1):89-99.

Baron, J.; Schmidt, T.; Hartman, M. 2009. Climate-induced changes in high elevation stream nitrate dynamics. Global Change Biology 15:1777-1789.

Barrett, S. and Arno, S. 1982. Indian fires as an ecological influence in the northern Rockies. Journal of Forestry 80:647-651.

Bartlein, P.; Whitlock, C.; Shafer, S. 1997. Future climate in the Yellowstone National Park region and its potential impact on vegetation. Conservation Biology 11(3):782-792.

Bartlein, P.; Anderson, K.; Anderson, P. [and others]. 1998. Paleoclimate simulations for North America over the past 21,000 years: features of the simulated climate and comparisons with paleoenvironmental data. Quaternary Science Reviews 17:549-585.

Bebi, P.; Kulakowski, D.; Veblen, T. 2003. Interactions between fire and spruce beetles in a subalpine Rocky Mountain forest landscape. Ecology 84(2):362-371.

Bell, J. 2009. Glacier meltwater contribution and streamflow variability in the Wind River Range, Wyoming. Thesis, University of Wyoming.

Bentz, B. 2005. Bark beetle outbreaks in western North America: causes and consequences. Bark Beetle Symposium. Snowbird, Utah, University of Utah Press.

Bentz, B.; Regniere, J.; Fettig, C. [and others]. 2010. Climate change and bark beetles of the western United States and Canada: direct and indirect effects. Bioscience 60(8):602-613.

Berger, A. 1978. Long-term variations of caloric insolation resulting from the earth's orbital elements. Quaternary Research 9(2):139-167.

Bethlahmy, N. 1974. More streamflow after a bark beetle epidemic. Journal of Hydrology 23:185-189.

Bigler, C.; Kulakowski, D.; Veblen, T. 2005. Multiple disturbance interactions and drought influence fire severity in Rocky Mountain subalpine forests. Ecology 86(11):3018-3029.

Bradley, B.; Oppenheimer, M.; Wilcove, D. 2009. Climate change and plant invasions: restoration opportunities ahead? Global Change Biology 15:1511-1521.

Bradley, B.; Blumenthal, D.; Wilcove, D. [and others]. 2010. Predicting plant invasions in an era of global change. Trends in Ecology and Evolution 25(5):310-318.

Breshears, D.; Cobb, N.; Rich, P. [and others]. 2005. Regional vegetation die-off in response to global-change type drought. Proceedings of the National Academy of Sciences, USA 102:15144-15148.

Brocoli, A. and Manabe, S. 1987. The influence of continental ice, atmospheric CO_2, and land albedo on the climate of the last glacial maximum. Climate Dynamics 1:87-99.

Brown, K.; Hansen, A.; Keane, R. [and others]. 2006. Complex interactions shaping aspen dynamics in the Greater Yellowstone Ecosystem. Landscape Ecology 21:933-951.

Brown, T. and Froemke, P. 2010. Risk of impaired condition of watersheds containing National Forest land. Gen. Tech. Rep. RMRS-GTR-251. Fort Collins, CO: U.S. Department of Agriculture, Forest Service, Rocky Mountain Research Station 57 p.

Brunelle, A.; Rehfeldt, G.; Bentz, B. [and others]. 2008. Holocene records of *Dendroctonus* bark beetles in high elevation pine forests of Idaho and Montana, USA. Forest Ecology and Management 255:836-846.

Burkett, V. and Kusler, J. 2000. Climate change: potential impacts and interactions in wetlands of the United States. Journal of the American Water Resources Association 36(2):313-320.

Burkett, V.; Wilcox, D.; Stottlemyer, R. [and others]. 2005. Nonlinear dynamics in ecosystem response to climatic change: case studies and policy implications. Ecological Complexity 2(4):357-394.

Cannone, N.; Sgorbati, S.; Guglielmin, M. 2007. Unexpected impacts of climate change on alpine vegetation. Frontiers in Ecology and the Environment 5(7):360-364.

Carroll, A.; Regniere, J.; Logan, J. [and others]. 2006. Impacts of climate change on range expansion by the mountain pine beetle. Victoria, British Columbia, Canada, Mountain Pine Beetle Initiative.

Cayan, D.; Redmond, K.; Riddle, L. 1999. ENSO and hydrologic extremes in the western United States. American Meteorological Society 12:2881-2893.

Cheesbrough, K.; Edmunds, J.; Tootle, G. [and others]. 2009. Estimated Wind River Range (Wyoming, USA) glacier melt water contributions to agriculture. Remote Sensing 1:818-828.

Chong, G.; Simonson, S.; Stohlgren, T. [and others]. 2001. Biodiversity: aspen stands have the lead, but will nonnative species take over? Proc. RMRS-P-18. Fort Collins, CO: U.S. Department of Agriculture, Forest Service, Rocky Mountain Research Station: 261-272.

Christensen, N.; Wood, A.; Voisin, N. [and others]. 2004. The effects of climate change on the hydrology and water resources of the Colorado River basin. Climatic Change 62:337-363.

Christensen, J.; Hewitson, B.; Busuioc, A. [and others]. 2007. Climate change 2007: the physical science basis. Contribution of Working Group I to the Fourth Assessment Report of the Intergovernmental Panel on Climate Change. Cambridge, United Kingdom, and New York, USA: Cambridge University Press.

Clark, G. 2010. Changes in patterns of streamflow from unregulated watersheds in Idaho, western Wyoming, and northern Nevada. Journal of the American Water Resources Association 46(3):486-497.

Cook, E.; Woodhouse, C.; Eakin, M. [and others]. 2004. Long-term aridity changes in the western United States. Science 306:1015-1018. DOI:10.1126/science.1102586.

Cook, N.; Rahel, F.; Hubert, W. 2010. Persistence of Colorado River cutthroat trout populations in isolated headwater streams of Wyoming. Transactions of the American Fisheries Society 139:1500-1510.

Copeland, H.; Tessman, S.; Girvetz, E. [and others]. 2010. A geospatial assessment on the distribution, condition, and vulnerability of Wyoming's wetlands. Ecological Indicators 10:869-879.

Cordell, H.K. and Overdevest, C. 2001. Footprints on the land: an assessment of demographic trends and the future of natural lands in the United States. United States: Sagamore Publishing.

Corn, P. 2007. Amphibians and disease: implications for conservation in the Greater Yellowstone Ecosystem. Yellowstone Science 15(2):11-16.

Cripps, C. and Eddington, L. 2005. Distribution of mycorrhizal types among alpine vascular plant families on the Beartooth Plateau, Rocky Mountains, U.S.A., in reference to large-scale patterns in arctic-alpine habitats. Arctic, Antarctic, and Alpine Research 37(2):177-188.

Cross, P.; Cole, E.; Dobson, A. [and others]. 2010. Probable causes of increasing brucellosis in free-ranging elk of the Greater Yellowstone Ecosystem. Ecological Applications 20(1):278-288.

Curtis, J. and Grimes, K. 2004. Wyoming Climate Atlas. Available: http://www.wrds.uwyo.edu/sco/climateatlas/toc html.

Dale, V. 1997. The relationship between land-use change and climate change. Ecological Applications 7(3):753-769.

Daly, C.; Halbleib, M.; Smith, J. [and others]. 2008. Physiographicaly sensitive mapping of climatological temperature and precipitation across the conterminous United States. International Journal of Climatology DOI:10.1002/joc.1688.

Danielopol, D.; Griebler, C.; Gunatilaka, A. [and others]. 2003. Present state and future prospects for groundwater ecosystems. Environmental Conservation 30(2):104-130.

DeRito, J.; Zale, A.; Shepard, B. 2010. temporal reproductive separation of fluvial Yellowstone cutthroat trout from rainbow trout and hybrids in the Yellowstone River. North American Journal of Fisheries Management 30:855-886.

Despain, D. 1987. The two climates of Yellowstone National Park. Proceedings of the Montana Academy of Sciences 47:11-20.

Dettinger, M.; Cayan, D.; Diaz, H. [and others]. 1998. North-south precipitation patterns in western North America on interannual-to-decadal timescales. Journal of Climate 11:3095-3111.

Dietz, H. and Edwards, P. 2006. Recognition that causal processes change during plant invasion helps explain conflicts in evidence. Ecology 87(6):1359-1367.

Diffenbaugh, N.; Sloan, L.; Snyder, M. [and others]. 2003. Vegetation sensitivity to global anthropogenic carbon dioxide emissions in a topographically complex region. Global Biogeochemical Cycles 17(2):1067-1080.

DiTomaso, J. 2000. Invasive weeds in rangelands: species, impacts, and management. Weed Science 48(2):255-265.

Dukes, J. and Mooney, H. 1999. Does global change increase the success of biological invaders? Trends in Ecology and Evolution 14(4):135-139.

Dullinger, S.; Dirnbock, T.; Grabherr, G. 2004. Modelling climate change-driven treeline shifts: relative effects of temperature increase, dispersal and invasibility. Journal of Ecology 92(2):241-252.

Durham, D. and Marlow, C. 2010. Aspen response to prescribed fire under managed cattle grazing and low elk densities in southwest Montana. Northwest Science 84(1):141-150.

Ellison, A.; Bank, M.; Clinton, B. [and others]. 2005. Loss of foundation species: consequences for the structure and dynamics of forested ecosystems. Frontiers in Ecology and Environment 3(9):479-486.

Elsner, M.; Cuo, L.; Voisin, N. [and others]. 2010. Implications of 21st Century climate change for the hydrology of Washington State. Climatic Change 102:225-260.

Erwin, K. 2009. Wetlands and global climate change: the role of wetland restoration in a changing world. Wetlands Ecology and Management 17:71-84.

Fahey, T.; Yavitt, J.; Pearson, J. [and others]. 1985. The nitrogen-cycle in lodgepole pine forests, southeastern Wyoming. Biogeochemistry 1(3):257-275.

Fall, P.; Davis, P.; Zielinski, G. 1995. Late quaternary vegetation and climate of the Wind-River Range, Wyoming. Quaternary Research 43(3):393-404.

Feely, R.; Sabine, C.; Lee, K. [and others]. 2004. Impact of anthropogenic CO2 on the CaCO3 system in oceans. Science 305:362-366.

Finlayson, C.M. and D'Cruz, R. 2005. Inland water systems. Chapter 20 of Ecosystems and human well-being: current state and trends. The Millennium Ecosystem Assessment, Volume I. United States, Island Press.

Flannigan, M.; Stocks, B.; Wotton, B. 2000. Climate change and forest fires. The Science of the Total Environments 262:221-229.

Flanagan, K.; McCauley, E.; Wrona, F. [and others]. 2003. Climate change: the potential for latitudinal effects on algal biomass in aquatic ecosystems. Canadian Journal of Fish and Aquatic Science 60:635-639.

Freiden, M. 2010. Treeline dynamics on the west slope of Pikes Peak. Thesis, Colorado Springs, CO; Colorado College. 43 p.

Gibson, K. 2006. Mountain pine beetle conditions in whitebark pine stands in the Greater Yellowstone Ecosystem, 2006. Numbered Report 06-03. Missoula, MT: U.S. Department of Agriculture, Forest Service, Northern Region.

Gosnell, H.; Haggerty, J.; Travis, W. 2006. Ownership change in the Greater Yellowstone Ecosystem, 1990-2001: implications for conservation. Society and Natural Resources 19:743-758.

Grace, J.; Berninger, F.; Nagy, L. 2002. Impacts of climate change on tree line. Annals of Botany 90:537-544.

Granshaw, F. and Fountain, A. 2006. Glacier simulations on-line. Available: http://glaciers.pdx.edu/Projects/LearnAboutGlaciers/GlacierModels/. Accessed June 24, 2010.

Graumlich, L.; Pisaric, M.; Waggoner, L. [and others]. 2003. Upper Yellowstone River flow and teleconnections with Pacific basin climate variability during the past three centuries. Climatic Change 59(1-2):245-262.

Gray, S.; Graumlich, L.; Betancourt, L. 2007. Annual precipitation in the Yellowstone National Park region since AD 1173. Quaternary Research 68(1):18-27.

Gray, S. and McCabe, G. 2010. A combined water balance and tree ring approach to understanding the potential hydrologic effects of climate change in the central Rocky Mountain region. Water Resources Research 46:1-13.

Gregory, J.; Scribner, N.; Toye, C. 2009. Movement of Yellowstone cutthroat trout in the Wind River watershed of Wyoming. Wyoming Game and Fish Department Report. Available: http://gf.state.wy.us/downloads/pdf/RegionalNews/LanYSC10.pdf.

Gude, P.; Hansen, A.; Rasker, R. [and others]. 2006. Rates and drivers of rural residential development in the Greater Yellowstone. Landscape and Urban Planning 77(1-2):131-151.

Gude, P.; Hansen, A.; Jones, D. 2007. Biodiversity consequences of alternative future land use scenarios in Greater Yellowstone. Ecological Applications 17(4):1004-1018.

Greater Yellowstone Science Learning Center [GYSLC]. 2008. Greater Yellowstone resource brief: climate. Available: http://www.greateryellowstonescience.org/subproducts/376/.

Hall, M. and Fagre, D. 2003. Modeled climate-induced glacier change in Glacier National Park, 1850-2100. Bioscience 53(2):131-140.

Halofsky, J. and Ripple, W. 2008. Linkages between wolf presence and aspen recruitment in the Gallatin elk winter range of southwestern Montana, USA. Forestry 196-207.

Hansen, A.; Neilson, R.; Dale, V. [and others]. 2001. Global change in forests: responses of species, communities, and biomes. Bioscience 51(9):765-779.

Hansen, A.; Rasker, R.; Maxwell, B. [and others] .2002. Ecological causes and consequences of demographic change in the new west. Bioscience 52(2):151-162.

Hansen, A. 2006. Yellowstone bioregional assessment: understanding the ecology and land use of Greater Yellowstone. Technical Report #2, Landscape Biodiversity Lab, Montana State University, Bozeman.

Hansen, A. and DeFries, R. 2007. Ecological mechanisms linking protected areas to surrounding lands. Ecological Applications 17(4):974-988.

Hansen, K. 2007. Yellowstone fires leave microbes nitrogen-hungry. Geotimes 52(5):12-13. Available: http://www.geotimes.org/may07/article html?id=nn_microbes html.

Haroldson, M.; Schwartz, C.; Kendall, K. [and others]. 2010. Genetic analysis of individual origins support the isolation of grizzly bears in the Greater Yellowstone Ecosystem. Ursus 21(1):1-13.

Hassan, R.; Scholes, R.; Ash, N. 2005. Ecosystems and human well-being: current state and trends: findings of the Condition and Trends Working Group. The Millennium Ecosystem Asssessment, Volume I. United States, Island Press.

Hatala, J.; Crabtree, R.; Halligan, K. [and others]. 2009. Landscape-scale patterns of forest pest and pathogen damage in the Greater Yellowstone Ecosystem. Remote Sensing of Environment DOI:10.1016/j.rse.2009.09.008.

Hauer, F.; Baron, J.; Campbell, D. [and others]. 1997. Assessment of climate change and freshwater ecosystems of the Rocky Mountains, USA and Canada. Hydrological Processes 11(8):903-924.

Heidel, B. and Rodemaker, E. 2008. Inventory of peatland systems in the Beartooth Mountains, Shoshone National Forest. Available: http://www.uwyo.edu/wynddsupport/docs/Reports/WYNDDReports/U08HEI02WYUS.pdf.

Helie, J.; Peters, D.; Tattrie, K. [and others]. 2005. Review and synthesis of potential hydrologic impacts of mountain pine beetle and related harvesting activities in British Columbia. Mountain Pine Beetle Initiative Working Paper 2005-03. Canadian Forest Service. Available: http://mpb.cfs nrcan.gc.ca.

Hessl, A. and Baker, W. 1997. Spruce and fire regeneration and climate in the forest-tundra ecotone of Rocky Mountain National Park, Colorado, U.S.A. Arctic and Alpine Research 29(2):173-183.

Hessl, A. and Graumlich, L. 2002. Interactive effects of human activities, herbivory and fire on quaking aspen (*Populus tremuloides*) age structures in western Wyoming. Journal of Biogeography 29:889-902.

Hicke, J.; Logan, J.; Powell, J. [and others]. 2006. Changing temperatures influence suitability for modeled mountain pine beetle (Dendroctonus ponderosae) outbreaks in the western United States. Journal of Geophysical Research-Biogeosciences 111, G02019, DOI:10.1029/2005JG000101.

Higuera, P.; Whitlock, C.; Gage, J. 2010. Linking tree-ring and sediment-charcoal records to reconstruct fire occurrence and area burned in subalpine forests of Yellowstone National Park, USA. The Holocene 21(2):327-341.

Hill, E.; Bergstrom, J.; Cordell, H.K. [and others]. 2009. Natural resource amenity service values and impacts in the U.S. Internet Research Information Series (IRIS). Available: http://warnell.forestry.uga.edu/nrrt/nsre/IRISDemo/IrisDemo2rpt.pdf. Historic Climate Network station data. Available: http://cdiac.ornl.gov/epubs/ndp/ushcn/access html.

Hobbs, N.; Galvin, K.; Stokes, C. [and others]. 2008. Fragmentation of rangelands: implications for humans, animals, and landscapes. Global Environmental Change 18(4):776-785.

Hoerling, M.; Lettenmaier, D.; Cayan, D. [and others]. 2009. Reconciling projections of Colorado River streamflow. Southwest Hydrology May/June Issue 8:20-21.

Hogg, E.; Brandt, J.; Kochtubajda, B. 2002. Growth and dieback of aspen forests in northwestern Alberta, Canada, in relation to climate and insects. Canadian Journal of Forest Research 32:823-932.

Hogg, E.; Brandt, J.; Michaelian, M. 2008. Impacts of a regional drought on the productivity, dieback, and biomass of western Canadian aspen forests. Canadian Journal of Forest Research 38:1373-1384.

Hollenbeck, J. and Ripple, W. 2007. Aspen and conifer heterogeneity effects on bird diversity in the northern Yellowstone Ecosystem. Western North American Naturalist 67 (1):92-101.

Hostetler, S. and Giorgi, F. 1995. Effects of a 2-Times-CO_2 climate on 2 large lake systems—Pyramid Lake, Nevada, and Yellowstone Lake, Wyoming. Global and Planetary Change 10(1-4):43-54.

Houston, Kent. 2011. Personal Communication. Soil Scientist, Shoshone National Forest.

Huerta, M.; Whitlock, C.; Yale, J. 2009. Holocene vegetation-fire-climate linkages in northern Yellowstone National Park, USA. Palaeogeography, Palaeoclimatology, Palaeoecology 271:170-181.

Hunter, T.; Tootle, G.; Piechota, T. 2006. Oceanic-atmospheric variability and western U.S. snowfall. Geophysical Research Letters 33:1-5.

Intergovernmental Panel on Climate Change [IPCC]. 2007a. Climate Change 2007: The physical science basis. Contribution of Working Group I to the Fourth Assessment Report of the Intergovernmental Panel on Climate Change. S. Solomon, D. Qin, M. Manning, Z. Chen, M. Marquis, K. Averyt, M. Tignor, and H. Miller. Cambridge University Press, Cambridge, United Kingdom and New York, NY, USA. 996 p.

Intergovernmental Panel on Climate Change [IPCC]. 2007b. Climate Change 2007: synthesis report. Contribution of Working Groups I, II and III to the Fourth Assessment Report of the Intergovernmental Panel on Climate Change. R. Pachauri and A. Reisinger. Geneva, Switzerland.

Isebrands, J.; McDonald, E.; Kruger, E. [and others]. 2001. Growth responses of *Populus tremuloides* clones to interacting elevated carbon dioxide and tropospheric ozone. Environmental Pollution 115:359-371.

Jenkins, M.; Hebertson, E.; Page, W. [and others]. 2008. Bark beetles, fuels, fires and implications for forest management in the Intermountain West. Forest Ecology and Management 254:16-34.

Jenkins, A. and Keeley, E. 2010. Bioenergetic assessment of habitat quality for stream-dwelling cutthroat trout (*Oncorhynchus clarkia bouvieri*) with implications for climate change and nutrient supplementation. Canadian Journal of Fish and Aquatic Science 67:371-385.

Jimenez, M.; Smith, D.; Stahler, D. [and others]. 2010. Wyoming wolf recovery 2009 annual report. WY-1 to WY-28 *in:* U.S. Fish and Wildlife Service Rocky Mountain Wolf Recovery 2009 Annual Report. Helena, MT: U.S. Fish and Wildlife Service, Ecological Services.

Johnson, J. 2008. State of the land—analysis of land use change in Montana and the 3 Regions. Available: http://fwp mt.gov/doingBusiness/reference/montanaChallenge/reports/landuse.html.

Joyce, L.; Aber, J.; McNulty, S. [and others]. 2001. Potential consequences of climate variability and change for the forests of the United States. National Assessment Synthesis Team (eds.). Chapter 17 (pp. 489-524). Climate Change Impacts on the United States. Cambridge University Press, Cambridge.

Joyce, L.; Blate, G.; Littell, J. [and others]. 2008a. National Forests. *in:* S. Julius, J. West, J. Baron, B. Griffith, L. Joyce, P. Kareiva, B. Keller, M. Palmer, C. Peterson, and J. Scott. Preliminary review of adaptation options for climate-sensitive ecosystems and resources. Synthesis and Assessment Product 4.4. A Report by the U.S. Climate Change Science Program and the Subcommittee on Global Change Research. Washington, DC: U.S. Environmental Protection Agency: 3-1 to 3-127.

Joyce, L.; Flather, C.; Koopman, M. 2008b. WHPRP final project report: 1.B:analysis of potential impacts of climate change on wildlife habitats in the U.S. Available: http://www.ncseonline.org/00/Batch/WHPRP/2007%20Final%20Reports/1B_ljoyce_WHPRP%20Final%20Report%20Project%20for%20web.pdf.

Jules, E.; Carroll, A.; Kauffman, M. 2010. The relationship of climate and growth of quaking aspen (*Populus tremuloides*) in Yellowstone National Park. Available: http://www humboldt.edu/cuca/documents/reports/CA-RWO81%20Final%20Report-1.pdf.

Kalra, A.; Piechota, T.; Davies R. [and others]. 2008. Changes in U.S. streamflow and western U.S. snowpack. Journal of Hydrologic Engineering 3(13):156-163.

Karl, T.; Melillo, J.; Peterson, T. 2009. Global climate change impacts in the United States. Cambridge University Press. Available: http://www.globalchange.gov/publications/reports/scientific-assessments/us-impacts/download-the-report.

Kashian, D.; Romme, W.; Tinker, D. [and others]. 2006. Carbon storage on landscapes with stand-replacing fires. Bioscience 56(7):598-606.

Kaushal, S.; Likens, G.; Joworski, N. 2010. Rising stream and river temperatures in the United States. Frontiers in Ecology and the Environment. DOI:10.1890/090037.

Keane, R. and Arno, S. 1993. Rapid decline of Whitebark Pine in western Montana: evidence from 20-year remeasurements. Western Journal of Applied Forestry 8(2):44-47.

Keane, R.; Ryan, K.; Veblen, T. 2002. Cascading effects of fire exclusion in Rocky Mountain Ecosystems: a literature review. Gen. Tech. Rep. RMRS-GTR-91. Fort Collins, CO: U.S. Department of Agriculture, Forest Service, Rocky Mountain Research Station.

Keane, R. and Parsons, R. 2010. Restoring whitebark pine forests of the northern Rocky Mountains, USA. Ecological Restoration 28(1):56-70.

Keleher, C. and Rahel, F. 1996. Thermal limits to salmonid distributions in the Rocky Mountain region and potential habitat loss due to global warming: a Geographic Information System (GIS) approach. Transactions of the American Fisheries Society 125(1):1-13.

Kendall, K. and Keane, R. 2001. Whitebark pine decline: infection, mortality and population trends. *in:* D. Tomback, S. Arno, and R. Keane. Whitebark pine communities: ecology and restoration. Washington, DC: Island Press: 221-242.

Klasner, F. and Fagre, D. 2002. A half century of change in alpine treeline patterns at Glacier National Park, Montana, U.S.A. Arctic, Antarctic, and Alpine Research 34(1):49-56.

Knowles, N. and Cayan, D. 2004. Elevational Dependence of Projected Hydrologic Changes in the San Francisco Estuary and Watershed. Climatic Change 62:319-336.

Knowles, N.; Dettinger, M.; Cayan, D.R. 2006. Trends in snowfall versus rainfall in the western United States. Journal of Climate 19: 4545-4559.

Korner, C.; Asshoff, R.; Bignucolo, O. [and others]. 2005. Carbon flux and growth in mature deciduous forest trees exposed to elevated CO_2. Science 309:1360-1362.

Koschel, C. 2010. The effects of climate change on algae in the Denver Metro area's drinking water reservoirs. Thesis, University of Denver.

Koteen, L. 2002. Climate change, whitebark pine, and grizzly bears in the Greater Yellowstone Ecosystem. Wildlife responses to climate change: North American case studies. S. Schneider and T. Root. Washington, DC, Island Press: 343-414.

Krimmel, R. 2002. Glaciers of the conterminous United States. U.S. Geological Survey Professional Paper 1386-J-2. Available: http://pubs.usgs.gov/pp/p1386j/us/westus-lores.pdf.

Krishnan, P.; Black, T.; Grant, N. [and others]. 2006. Impact of changing soil moisture distribution on net ecosystem productivity of a boreal aspen forest during and following drought. Agricultural and Forest Meteorology 139:208-223.

Kruse, C.; Hubert, W.; Rahel, F. 1997. Geomorphic Influences on the Distribution of Yellowstone cutthroat trout in the Absaroka Mountains, Wyoming. Transactions of the American Fisheries Society 126(3):418-427.

Kulakowski, D.; Veblen, T.; Bebi, P. 2003 Effects of fire and spruce beetle outbreak legacies on the disturbance regime of a subalpine forest in Colorado. Journal of Biogeography 30:1445-1456.

Kulakowski, D. and Veblen, T. 2007. Effect of prior disturbances on the extent and severity of wildfire in Colorado subalpine forests. Ecology 88(3):759-769.

Kunkel, K.; Easterling, D.; Redmond, K. [and others]. 2003. Temporal variations of extreme precipitation events in the United States: 1895-2000. Geophysical Research Letters 30(17):1990.

Kurz, W.; Dymond, C.; Stinson, G. [and others]. 2008. Mountain pine beetle and forest carbon feedback to climate change. Nature 452(7190):987-990.

Kutzbach, J. and Guetter, P. 1986. The influence of changing orbital parameters and surface boundary conditions on climate simulations for the past 18,000 years. Journal of the Atmospheric Sciences 43(16):1726-1759.

LaMalfa, E. and Ryle, R. 2008. Differential snowpack accumulation and water dynamics in aspen and conifer communities: implications for water yield and ecosystem function. Ecosystems 11:569-581.

Larson, E. and Kipfmueller, K. 2010. Patterns in whitebark pine regeneration and their relationships to biophysical site characteristics in southwest Montana, central Idaho, and Oregon, USA. Canadian Journal of Forest Research 40:476-487.

Lawler, J.; Shafer, S.; White, D. [and others]. 2009. Projected climate-induced faunal changes in the Western Hemisphere. Ecology 90(3):588-597.

Leung, L. and Qian, Y. 2009. Atmospheric rivers induce heavy precipitation and flooding in the western U.S. simulated by the WRF regional climate model. Geophysical Research Letters 36, L03820. DOI:10.1029/2008GL036445.

Lewis, D. and Huggard, D. 2010. A model to quantify the effects of mountain pine beetle on equivalent clearcut area. Watershed Management Bulletin 13(2):42-51.

Liciardi, J. and Pierce, K. 2008. Cosmogenic exposure-age chronologies of Pindale and Bull Lake glaciations in Greater Yellowstone and the Teton Range. Quaternary Science Reviews 27:814-831.

Lindroth, R.; Kinney, K.; Platz, C. 1993. Responses of diciduous trees to elevated atmospheric CO_2: productivity, phytochemistry, and insect performance. Ecology 74(3):763-777.

Loehman, R.; Corrow, A.; Keane, R. 2010. Modeling climate changes and wildfire interactions: effects on whitebark pine (Pinus albicaulis) and implications for restoration, Glacier National Park, Montana, USA. in: R. Keane; D. Tomback; M. Murray; and C. Smith. 2011. The future of high-elevation, five-needle white pines in Western North America: Proceedings of the High Five Symposium; 28-30 June 2010; Missoula, MT. Proc. RMRS-P-63. Fort Collins, CO: U.S. Department of Agriculture, Forest Service, Rocky Mountain Research Station. 376 p.

Logan, J. and Powell, J. 2001. Ghost forests, global warming, and the mountain pine beetle (Coleoptera: Scolytidae). American Entomologist 47(3):160-172.

Logan, J.; Macfarlane, W.; Willcox, L. 2010. Whitebark pine vulnerability to climate-driven mountain pine beetle disturbance in the Greater Yellowstone Ecosystem. Ecological Applications 20(4):895-902.

Loomis, J. and Crespi, J. 1999. Estimated effects of climate change on selected outdoor recreation activities in the United States. in: R. Mendelsohn, J. Neumann. The impact of climate change on the United States economy. Cambridge University Press, Cambridge: 289-314.

Love, L. 1955. The effect on stream flow of killing of spruce and pine by the Engelmann spruce beetle. American Geophysical Union Transactions 36(1):113-118.

Lowell, E.; Rapp, V.; Haynes, R. [and others]. 2010. Effects of fire, insect, and pathogen damage on wood quality of dead and dying western conifers. Gen. Tech. Rep. PNW-GTR-816. Corvallis, OR: U.S. Department of Agriculture, Forest Service, Pacific Northwest Research Station. 73 p.

Lueneburg, S. 2007. Physical geography of Yellowstone National Park. Available: http://www.glendale.edu/geo/reed/physical/Physical_Geography_of_Yellowstone_National_Park.pdf.

Lukas, J. and Gordon, E. 2010. Impacts of the mountain pine beetle infestation on the hydrologic cycle and water quality: a symposium report and summary of the latest science. Intermountain West Climate Summary 6(3):1-4.

Luo, Y.; Su, B.; Currie, W. [and others]. 2004. Progressive nitrogen limitation of ecosystem responses to rising atmospheric carbon dioxide. Bioscience 54(8):731-739.

Lyford, M.; Jackson, S.; Betancourt, J. [and others]. 2003. Influence of landscape structure and climate variability on a late Holocene plant migration. Ecological Monographs 73(4):567-583.

Lynch, H.; Renkin, R.; Crabtree, R. [and others]. 2006. The influence of previous mountain pine beetle (Dendroctonus ponderosae) activity on the 1988 Yellowstone fires. Ecosystems 9(8):1318-1327.

MacDonald, L. and Stednick, J. 2003. Forest and water: a state of the art review for Colorado. Colorado Water Resources Research Institute, Completion Report No. 196.

Malanson, G.; Butler, D.; Fagre, D. [and others]. 2007. Alpine treeline of western North America: linking organisms-to-landscape dynamics. Physical Geography 28(5):378-396.

Manier, D. and Laven, R. 2002. Changes in landscape pattern associated with the persistence of aspen (Populus tremuloides Michx.) on the western slope of the Rocky Mountains, Colorado. Forest Ecology and Management 167:263-284.

Mantua, N.; Hare, S.; Zhang, Y. [and others]. 1997. A Pacific interdecadal climate oscillation with impacts on salmon production. Bulletin of the American Meteorological Society 78(6):1069-1079.

Mattson, D.; Blanchard, B.; Knight, R. 1992. Yellowstone grizzly bear mortality, human habituation, and whitebark pine seed crops. Journal of Wildlife Management 56(3):432-442.

McCool, S. 2001. Quaking aspen and the human experince: dimensions, issues, and challenges. Proc. RMRS-P-18. Fort Collins, CO: U.S. Department of Agriculture, Forest Service, Rocky Mountain Research Station: 147-161.

McCullough, D.; Werner, R.; Neumann, D. 1998. Fire and insects in northern and boreal forest ecosystems of North America. Annual Review of Entomology 43(1):107-127.

McMenamin, S.; Hadly, E.; Wright, C. 2008. Climatic change and wetland desiccation cause amphibian decline in Yellowstone National Park. Proceedings of the National Academy of Sciences of the United States of America 105(44):16,988-16,993.

McNab, W.; Cleland, D.; Freeouf, J. [and others]. 2005. Description of ecological subregions: sections of the conterminous United States [CD-ROM]. Washington, DC: U.S. Department of Agriculture, Forest Service. 80 p.

McWethy, D.; Gray, S.; Higuera, P. [and others]. 2010. Climate and terrestrial ecosystem change in the U.S. Rocky Mountains and Upper Columbia Basin: Historical and future perspectives for natural resource management. Natural Resource Report NPS/GRYN/NRR-2010/260. Fort Collins, CO: National Park Service.

Meehl, G.; Cover, C.; Delworth, T. [and others]. 2007. The WCRP CMIP3 multimodel data set. Bulletin of the American Meteorological Society September 2007:1383-1394.

Mellman-Brown, S. 2002. The regeneration of whitebark pine in the timberline ecotone of the Beartooth Plateau, Montana and Wyoming. Dissertation, Westfälischen Wilhelms-Universität Münster.

Menlove, J. 2008. Forest resources of the Shoshone National Forest. Fort Collins, CO: U.S. Department of Agriculture, Forest Service, Rocky Mountain Research Station. Available: http://www fs fed.us/rm/ogden/pdfs/shoshone.pdf.

Meyer, G.; Wells, S.; Balling, R. [and others]. 1992. Response of alluvial systems to fire and climate change in Yellowstone National Park. Letters to Nature 357:147-150.

Meyer, C.; Knight, D.; Dillon, G. 2006. Historic variability for the upland vegetation of the Shoshone National Forest, Wyoming. U.S. Department of Agriculture, Forest Service, Lakewood, CO. Agreement Number 1102-0003-98-043.

Millenium Ecosystem Assessment [MEA]. 2005. Ecosystems and human well-being: our human planet: summary for decision makers. Washington, DC, Island Press.

Miller, C. and Waits, L. 2003. The history of effective population size and genetic diversity in the Yellowstone grizzly (*Ursus arctos*): implications for conservation. Proceedings of the National Academy of Sciences of the United States of America 100(7):4334-4339.

Miller, C. 2006. Wilderness fire management in a changing world. International Journal of Wilderness 12(1):18-22.

Millspaugh, S.; Whitlock, C.; Bartlein, P. 2000. Variations in fire frequency and climate over the past 17,000 yr in central Yellowstone National Park. Geology 28:211-214.

Mitchell, J. and Johns, T. 1997. On modification of global warming by sulphate aerosols. Journal of Climate 10:245-267.

Mock, C. 1996. Climatic controls and spatial variations of precipitation in the western United States. Journal of Climate 9(5):1111-1125.

Moore, R.; Fleming, S.; Menounos, B. [and others]. 2009. Glacier change in western North America: influences on hydrology, geomorphic hazards and water quality. Hydrological Processes 23(1):42-61.

Morelli, T. and Carr, S. 2011. A review of the potential effects of climate change on quaking aspen (*Populus tremuloides*) in the western United States and a new tool for surveying sudden aspen decline. Res. Pap. PSW-RP-235. Albany, CA: U.S. Department of Agriculture, Forest Service, Pacific Southwest Research Station. 31 p.

Morgan, J.; Milchunas, D.; LeCain, D. [and others]. 2007. Carbon dioxide enrichment alters plant community structure and accelerates shrub growth in the shortgrass steppe. Proceedings of the National Academy of Sciences 104(37):14724-14729.

Morris, D. and Walls, M. 2009. Climate change and outdoor recreation. resources for the future. Available: http://www rff.org/RFF/Documents/RFF-BCK-ORRG_ClimateChange.pdf.

Mote, P.; Hamlet, A.; Clark, M. [and others]. 2005. Declining mountain snowpack in western North America. Bulletin of the American Meteorological Society 86:39-49.

Murdoch, P.; Baron, J.; Miller, T. 2000. Potential effects of climate change on surface-water quality in North America. Journal of the American Water Resources Association 36(2):347-366.

Naftz, D.; Susong, D.; Schuster, P. [and others]. 2002. Ice core evidence of rapid air temperature increases since 1960 in alpine areas of the Wind River Range, Wyoming, United States. Journal of Geophysical Research-Atmospheres 107(D13).

National Invasive Species Information Center [NISIC]. 2010. What is an invasive species? Available: http://www.invasivespeciesinfo.gov/whatis.shtml.

National Ocean and Atmospheric Administration [NOAA]. 2010. Climate Division data Available: http://www.esrl noaa.gov/psd/data/timeseries/.

National Park Service [NPS]. 2009. Yellowstone resources and issues: climate change. Yellowstone Resources and Issues. L. Young. Mammoth Hot Springs, Wyoming, NPS Division of Interpretation, Yellowstone National Park.

Natural Resource Conservation Service. [NRCS]. 2010. SNOTEL data. Available: http://www.wcc nrcs.usda.gov/snotel/Wyoming/wyoming html.

Neff, J.; Ballantyne, A.; Farmer, G. [and others]. 2008. Increasing eolean dust deposition in the western United States linked to human activity. Nature Geoscience 1:189-95.

Norby, R.; DeLucia, E.; Gielen, B. [and others]. 2005. Forest response to elevated CO_2 is conserved across a broad range of productivity. Proceedings of the National Academy of Sciences 102(50):18052-18056.

Noss, R. 2001. Beyond Kyoto: forest management in a time of rapid climate change. Conservation Biology 15(3):578-590.

Ohlemuller, R.; Anderson, B.; Araujo, M. [and others]. 2008. The coincidence of climatic and species rarity: high risk to small-range species from climate change. Biology Letters 4:568-572.

Oswald, E. and Wohl, E. 2008. Wood-mediated geomorphic effects of a jökulhlaup in the Wind River Mountains, Wyoming. Geomorphology 100(3-4):549-562.

Painter, T.; Barrett, A.; Landry, C. [and others]. 2007. Impact of disturbed desert soils on duration of mountain snow cover. Geophysical Research Letters 34: L12502. DOI:10.1029/2007GL030284.

Painter, T.; Deems, J.; Belnap, J. [and others]. 2010. Response of Colorado river runoff to dust radiative forcing in snow. Proceedings of the National Academy of Science 107(40):17125-17130.

Parker, T.; Clancy, K.; Mathiasen, R. 2006. Interaction among fire, insects and pathogens in coniferous forests of the interior western United States and Canada. Agriculture and Forest Entomology 8:167-189.

Parmenter, A.; Hansen, A.; Kennedy, R. [and others]. 2003. Land use and land cover change in the Greater Yellowstone Ecosystem: 1975-1995. Ecological Applications 13(3):687-703.

Parmesan, C. 2006. Ecological and evolutionary responses to recent climate change. Annual Review of Ecology, Evolution, and Systematics 37:637-669.

Parmesan, C. 2007. Influences of species, latitudes and methodologies on estimates of phonological response to global warming. Global Change Biology 13:1860-1872.

Parton, W.; Ojima, D.; Schimel, D. 1994. Environmental change in grasslands: asssessment using models. Climatic Change 28:111-141.

Penuelas, J.; Ritishauser, T.; Filella, I. 2009. Phenology feedbacks on climate change. Science 324:887-888.

Pepin, N. and Lundquist, J. 2008. Temperature trends at high elevations: patterns across the globe. Geophysical Research Letters Vol. 35, L14701. DOI:10.1029/2008GL034026.

Perala, D. 1990. Quaking aspen (*Populus tremuloides* Michx.). *in*: Silvics of North America: II. Deciduous. R.M. Burns and B.H. Honkala (tech. cords.). Agric. Handb. U.S. Department of Agriculture: 555-569.

Pierce, W. 1961. Permafrost and thaw depressions in a peat deposit in the Beartooth Mountains, Northwestern Wyoming. U.S. Geological Survey, Professional Paper 424-B.

Pochop, L.; Marston, R.; Kerr, G. [and others]. 1990. Glacial icemelt in the Wind River Range, Wyoming. watershed planning and analysis in action, symposium proceedings of IR conference, Durango, CO: American Society of Civil Engineers.

Polley, H.; Mayeux, H.; Johnson, H. [and others]. 1997. Viewpoint: atmospheric CO_2, soil water, and shrub/grass ratios on rangelands. Journal of Range Management 50(3):278-284.

Potts, D. 1984: Hydrologic impacts of a large-scale mountain pine beetle (Dendroctonous ponderosae Hopkins) epidemic. Water Resources Bulletin 20(3):373-377.

Powell, S. and Hansen, A. 2007. Conifer cover increase in the Greater Yellowstone Ecosystem: frequency, rates, and spatial variation. Ecosystems 10(2):204-216.

Power, T. 1991. Ecosystem preservation and the economy in the Greater Yellowstone Area. Conservation Biology 5(3):395-404.

Radeloff, V.; Stewart, S.; Hawbaker, T. [and others]. 2010. Housing growth in and near United States protected areas limits their conservation value. Proceedings of the National Academy of Sciences 107(2):940-945.

Rahel, F. and Olden, J. 2008. Assessing the effects of climate change on aquatic invasive species. Conservation Biology 22(3):521-533.

Rasker, R. and Hansen, A. 2000. Natural ammenities and population growth in the Greater Yellowstone Ecosystem. Human Ecology Review 7(2):30-40.

Rasmussen, E. and Wallace, J. 1983. Meterological aspects of the El Nino/southern oscillation. Science 222(4629):1195-1202.

Ray, A.; Barsugli, J.; Averyt, K. [and others]. 2008. Climate change in Colorado: a synthesis to support water resources management and adaptation. Available: http://cwcb.state.co.us/public-information/ publications/Documents/ReportsStudies/ClimateChangeReportFull.pdf.

Ray, A.; Barsugli, J.; Wolter, K. [and others]. 2010. Rapid-response climate assessment to support the FWS status review of the American pika. Available: http://www.esrl noaa.gov/psd/news/2010/pdf/pika_report_final.pdf.

Regonda, S.; Rajagopalan, B.; Clark, M. [and others]. 2005. Seasonal cycle shifts in hydroclimatology over the western United States. Journal of Climate 18:372-384.

Rehfeldt, G.; Ferguson, D.; Crookston, N. 2009. Aspen, climate, and sudden decline in western USA. Forest Ecology and Management 258:2353-2364.

Rhoades, C.; Elder, K.; Greene, E. 2010. The influence of an extensive dust event on snow chemistry in the southern Rocky Mountains. Arctic, Antarctic, and Alpine Research. 42(1):98-105.

Richardson, R. and Loomis, J. 2004. Adaptive recreation planning and climate change: a contingent visitation approach. Ecological Economics 50(1-2):83-99.

Rieman, B. and Isaak, D. 2010. Climate change, aquatic ecosystems, and fishes in the Rocky Mountain West: implications and alternatives for management. Gen. Tech. Rep. RMRS-GTR-250. Fort Collins, CO: U.S. Department of Agriculture, Forest Service, Rocky Mountain Research Station. 46 p.

Romme, W. and Turner, M. 1991. Implications of global climate change for biogeographic patterns in the Greater Yellowstone Ecosystem. Conservation Biology 5(3):373-386.

Romme, W.; Turner, M.; Wallace, L. [and others]. 1995. Aspen, elk, and fire in northern Yellowstone Park. Ecology 76(7):2097-2106.

Romme, W.; Clement, J.; Hicke, J. [and others]. 2006. Recent forest insect outbreaks and fire risk in Colorado forests: a brief synthesis of relevant research. Colorado State University, Fort Collins, CO: 24 p.

Romme, W.; Tinker, D.; Stakes, G. [and others]. 2009. Does inorganic nitrogen limit plant growth 3-5 years after fire in a Wyoming, USA, lodgepole pine forest? Forest Ecology and Management 257(3):829-835.

Root, T. and Schneider, S. 2002. Climate change: overview and implications for wildlife. Wildlife responses to climate change: North American case studies. Washington, DC, Island Press. 437 p.

Rowland, M.; Suring, L.; Tausch, R. [and others]. 2008. Characteristics of Western Juniper Encroachment into Sagebrush Communities in Central Oregon. La Grande, OR 97850: U.S. Department of Agriculture, Forest Service, Forestry and Range Sciences Laboratory.

Ryan, M.; Archer, S.; Birdsey, R. [and others]. 2008. Land Resources: forests and arid lands. The effects of climate change on agriculture, land resources, water resources, and biodiversity in the United States. A report by the U.S. Climate Change Science Program and the Subcommittee on Global Change Research, Washington, DC: 362.

Schlaepfer, D.; Lauenroth, W.; Bradford, B. 2011. Effects of ecohydrological variables on current and future ranges, local suitability patterns, and model accuracy in big sagebrush. Ecohydrology. DOI: 10.1002/eco.238.

Schoennagel, T.; Veblen, T.; Romme, W. 2004. The interaction of fire, fuels, and climate across Rocky Mountain forests. Bioscience 54:661-676.

Schrag, A.; Bunn, A.; Graumlich, L. 2008. Influence of bioclimatic variables on tree-line conifer distribution in the Greater Yellowstone Ecosystem: implications for species of conservation concern. Journal of Biogeography 35:698-710.

Schwartz, C.; Haroldson, M.; White, G. 2006. Study area and methods for collecting and analyzing demographic data on grizzly bears in the Greater Yellowstone Ecosystem. in: C. Schwartz; M. Haroldson; G. White. [and others]. Temporal, spatial and environmental influences on the demographics of grizzly bears in the Greater Yellowstone Ecosystem. Wildlife Monographs 161:9-15.

Schwartz, C.; Haroldson, M.; White, G. 2010. Hazards affecting grizzly bear survival in the Greater Yellowstone Ecosystem. Journal of Wildlife Management 74(4):654-667.

Shafer, S.; Bartlein, P.; Thompson, R. 2001. Potential changes in the distributions of western North America tree and shrub taxa under future climate scenarios. Ecosystems 4(3):200-215.

Sharma, S.; Jackson, D.; Minns, C. [and others]. 2007. Will northern fish populations be in hot water because of climate change? Global Change Biology 13:2052-2064.

Simard, M.; Powell, E.; Griffin, J. [and others]. 2008. annotated bibliography for forest managers on fire-bark beetle interactions. U.S. Department of Agriculture, Forest Service, Western Wildlands Environmental Threats Assessment Center. Available: http://www.colorado.edu/geography/class_homepages/geog_4430_s09/Simard_Beetle-FireInteractionsBiblio_08.pdf.

Simard, M. 2010. Bark beetle-fire-forest interactions in the Greater Yellowstone Ecosystem. Dissertation, University of Wisconsin.

Smith, W.; Germino, M.; Johnson, D. [and others]. 2009. The altitude of alpine treeline: a bellwether of climate change effects. The Botanical Review 75:163-190.

Smithwick, E.; Turner, M.; Mack, M. [and others]. 2005. Postfire soil N cycling in northern conifer forests affected by severe, stand-replacing wildfires. Ecosystems 8(2):163-181.

Smithwick, E.; Ryan, M.; Kashian, D. [and others]. 2009. Modeling the effects of fire and climate change on carbon and nitrogen storage in lodgepole pine (*Pinus contorta*) stands. Global Change Biology 15(3):535-548.

Stednick, J. and Jensen, R. 2007. Effects of pine beetle infestations on water yield and water quality at the watershed scale in northern Colorado. Report as of FY2007 for 2007CO153B, Colorado Water Resources Research Institute.

Steele, R.; Pfister, R.; Ryker, R. [and others]. 1981. Forest habitat types of central Idaho. Gen. Tech. Rep. INT-114. Ogden, UT: U.S. Department of Agriculture, Forest Service, Intermountain Forest and Range Experiment Station. 138 p.

Steltzer, H. and Post, E. 2009. Seasons and life cycles. Science 324:886-887.

Steltzer, H.; Landry, C.; Painter, T. [and others]. 2009. Biological consequences of earlier snowmelt from desert dust deposition in alpine landscapes. Proceedings of the National Academy of Sciences 106(28):11629-11634.

Stewart, I.; Cayan, D.; Dettinger, M. 2004. Changes in snowmelt runoff timing in western North America under a 'business as usual' climate change scenario. Climatic Change 62:217-232.

Stewart, I.; Cayan, D.; Dettinger, M. 2005. Changes toward earlier streamflow timing in western North America. Journal of Climate 18:1136-1155.

Stonefeldt, M.; Fontaine, T.; Hotchkiss, R. 2000. Impacts of climate change on water yields in the Upper Wind River Basin. Journal of the American Water Resources Association 36(2):321-336.

Story, M.; Shea, J.; Svalberg, T. [and others]. 2005. Greater Yellowstone Area air quality assessment update. Greater Yellowstone Clean Air Partnership. Available: http://www.nps.gov/yell/planyourvisit/upload/GYA_AirQuality_Nov_2005.pdf.

Swanson, C. 2008. Montana challenge: remaining the last best place for fish and wildlife in a changing west. 8th Biennial Scientific Conference Proceedings Greater Yellowstone Public Lands: 170-177. Available: http://www.nps.gov/yell/naturescience/upload/05.pdf.

Taylor, D.; Foulke, T.; Coupal, R. 2008. An economic profile of the Shoshone National Forest (DRAFT): prepared in support of the Shoshone National Forest plan revision process. University of Wyoming, Department of Agricultural and Applied Economics.

Tomback, D. and Resler, L. 2007. Invasive pathogens at alpine treeline: consequences for treeline dynamics. Physical Geography 28:397-418.

Troendle, C. and Nankervis, J. 2000 Estimating additional water yield from changes in management of National Forests in the North Platte Basin. Report to the U.S. Bureau of Reclamation. Available: http://www.fs.usda.gov/Internet/FSE_DOCUMENTS/stelprdb5167187.pdf.

Turner, M. and Romme, W. 1994. Landscape dynamics in crown fire ecosystems. Landscape Ecology 9(1):59-77.

Turner, M.; Romme, W.; Gardner, R. 1999. Prefire heterogeneity, fire severity, and early postfire plant reestablishment in subalpine forests of Yellowstone National Park, Wyoming. International Journal of Wildland Fire 9(0):21-36.

Turner, M.; Smithwick, E.; Metzger, K. [and others]. 2007. Inorganic nitrogen availability after severe stand-replacing fire in the Greater Yellowstone Ecosystem. Proceedings of the National Academy of Sciences of the United States of America 104(12):4782-4789.

Tweit, S. and Houston, K. 1980. Grassland and shrubland habitat types of the Shoshone National Forest. U.S. Department of Agriculture, Forest Service, Rocky Mountain Region, Shoshone National Forest.

United Stated Department of Agriculture [USDA]. 2010 Wyoming invasive species plant list. Available: http://plants.usda.gov/java/noxious?rptType=Stateandstatefips=56.

United States Bureau of Reclamation [USBR]. 2007a. Buffalo Bill. Available: http://www.usbr.gov/projects//ImageServer?imgName=Doc_1240933690814.pdf.

United States Bureau of Reclamation [USBR]. 2007b. Shoshone Power Plant Performance Report. Available: http://www.usbr.gov/projects//ImageServer?imgName=Doc_1240942423904.pdf.

United States Census. 2010. Available: http://2010.census.gov/2010census/data/.

United States Department of Agriculture, Forest Service [USDA Forest Service]. Shoshone Fire and RIS databases. 1970-2000. Cody, WY: U.S. Department of Agriculture, Forest Service, Rocky Mountain Region, Shoshone National Forest.

United States Department of Agriculture, Forest Service [USDA Forest Service]. 2008a. Watershed assessment of the Shoshone National Forest, Cody, WY. Cody, WY: U.S. Department of Agriculture, Forest Service, Rocky Mountain Region, Shoshone National Forest.

United States Department of Agriculture, Forest Service [USDA Forest Service]. 2008b. Assessment of recent bark beetle outbreaks on the Shoshone National Forest. biological evaluation. RCSC-08-02. Prepared by K. Allen and J. Ross. Cody, WY: U.S. Department of Agriculture, Forest Service, Rocky Mountain Region, Shoshone National Forest.

United States Department of Agriculture, Forest Service [USDA Forest Service]. 2009a. Current bark beetle activity in Wyoming from the 2007 aerial detection survey. Cody, WY: U.S. Department of Agriculture, Forest Service, Rocky Mountain Region, Shoshone National Forest.

United States Department of Agriculture, Forest Service [USDA Forest Service]. 2009b. Ecosystem diversity report. Cody, WY: U.S. Department of Agriculture, Forest Service, Rocky Mountain Region, Shoshone National Forest.

United States Department of Agriculture, Forest Service [USDA Forest Service]. 2009c. Comprehensive evaluation report: Shoshone National Forest, Cody, WY. Cody, WY: U.S. Department of Agriculture, Forest Service, Rocky Mountain Region, Shoshone National Forest.

United States Department of Agriculture, Forest Service [USDA Forest Service]. 2011a. Forest plan monitoring report for fiscal year 2009 Shoshone National Forest. Cody, WY: U.S. Department of Agriculture, Forest Service, Rocky Mountain Region, Shoshone National Forest. Available: http://www.fs.usda.gov/Internet/FSE_DOCUMENTS/stelprdb5285618.pdf.

United States Department of Agriculture, Forest Service [USDA Forest Service]. 2011b. 2010 Bark Beetle Aerial Detection Survey of the Shoshone National Forest, Cody, WY. Cody, WY: U.S. Department of Agriculture, Forest Service, Rocky Mountain Region, Shoshone National Forest.

United States Environmental Protection Agency [U.S. EPA]. 2008. Effects of climate change on aquatic invasive species and implications for management and research. National Center for Environmental Assessment, Washington, DC. EPA/600/R-08/014. Available from the National Technical Information Service, Springfield, VA. Available: http://www.epa.gov/ncea.

United States Environmental Protection Agency [U.S. EPA]. 2010. Climate change indicators in the United States. Available: http://www.epa.gov/climatechange/indicators/pdfs/ClimateIndicators_full.pdf.

United States Geological Survey [USGS]. 1989. W 2375. Wyoming floods and droughts. *in:* S. Druse. National water summary 1988-89. Hydrologic events and floods and droughts, R. Paulson, E. Chase, R. Roberts, and D. Moody (comps.). 1991: 575-582. Available: http://onlinepubs.er.usgs.gov/djvu/WSP/wsp_2375.djvu.

United States Geological Survey [USGS]. 2010. Wyoming non-indiginous aquatic species. Available: http://nas.er.usgs.gov/queries/SpeciesList.aspx?Group=andSortby=1andstate=WY.

United States Geological Survey National Water Information System [USGS NWIS]. 2010. Streamflow data. Available: http://waterdata.usgs.gov/wy/nwis/rt.

Van Kirk, R.; Battle, L.; Schrader, W. 2010. Modelling competition and hybridization between native cutthroat trout and nonnative rainbow and hybrid trout. Journal of Biological Dynamics 4(2):158-175.

Vitousek, P.; Aber, J.; Howarth, R. [and others]. 1997. Human alteration of the global nitrogen cycle: sources and consequences. Ecological Applications 7(3):737-750.

Walther, G.; Sascha, B.; Conradin, B. 2005. Trends in the upward shift of alpine plants. Journal of Vegetation Science 16(5):541-548.

Water Resource Data System points of diversion. 2007. GIS data Available: http://waterplan.state.wy.us/plan/statewide/gis/gis.html.

Watson, T.; Barnett, A.; Gray, S. [and others]. 2009. Reconstructed streamflows for the headwaters of the Wind River, Wyoming, United States. Journal of the American Water Resources Association 45(1):224-236.

Webb, B. and Noblis, F. 2007. Long-term changes in river temperature and the influence of climatic and hydrological factors. Hydrological Sciences 52(1):74-85.

Westerling, A.; Hidalgo, H.; Cayan, D. [and others]. 2006. Warming and earlier spring increase in western U.S. forest wildfire activity. Science 313:940-943.

Western Regional Climate Center. 2010. COOP climate station data. Available: http://www.wrcc.dri.edu/summary/Climsmwy.html.

White, P.; Proffitt, K.; Mech, L. [and others]. 2010. Migration of northern Yellowstone elk: implications of spatial structuring. Journal of Mammalogy 91(4):827-837.

Whitlock, C. 1993. Postglacial vegetation and climate of Grand-Teton and southern-Yellowstone-National-Parks. Ecological Monographs 63(2):173-198.

Whitlock, C. and Bartlein, P. 1993. Spatial variations of holocene climatic change in the Yellowstone Region. Quaternary Research 39(2):231-238.

Whitlock, C.; Shafer, S.; Marlon, J. [and others]. 2003. The role of climate and vegetation change in shaping past and future fire regimes in the northwestern US and the implications for ecosystem management. Forest Ecology and Management 178(1-2):5-21.

Wilmers, C. and Getz, W. 2005. Gray wolves as climate change buffers in Yellowstone. PLoS Biology 3(4):571-576.

Wilmers, C. and Post, E. 2006. Predicting the influence of wolf-provided carrion on scavenger community dynamics under climate change scenarios. Global Change Biology 12:403-409.

Winter, T. 2000. The vulnerability of wetlands to climate change: a hydrologic landscape perspective. Journal of the American Water Resources Association 36(2):305-311.

Wyoming Game and Fish. 2008. Annual big game herd reports. Available: http://gf.state.wy.us/wildlife/biggamejcr2008/index.asp.

Wyoming Game and Fish. 2010. Non-native fish species. Available: http://gf.state.wy.us/fish/fishing/stats/nonnative.asp.

Wyoming State Engineers Office. 2010, Goundwater well GIS data. Available: http://wygl.wygisc.org/wygeolib/catalog/browse/browse.page.

Xie, F. 2008. Disease and behavior dynamics for brucellosis in elk and cattle in the Greater Yellowstone Area. Thesis, Michigan State University.

Appendix Tables.

Table 1. □istoric □□i□□te □et□ or□ St□tio□s □se□ i□ t□is re□ort □□ro□ □tt□□□□c□i□c.or□□.□□e□□□s□□□□□□s□c□□□s□c□.□t□□□.

Station name	ID number	Elevation	Period of record	Latitude	Longitude
As□to□□ □□□□□o	100470	□□64	1□□□-□rese□t	44.042□	-111.27□□
□er□□ □□□□□o	100□0□	□□61	1□□□-□rese□t	42.0□□□	-111.□□□0
G□ce□□□□□o	10□7□2	□□4□	1□□□-□rese□t	42.□□00	-111.74□7
□i□to□ □□□□□i□ St□tio□□ □□□□o	10□27□	□□2□	1□□□-□rese□t	42.12□1	111.□1□□
□o□e□□□□ Mo□t□□□	241044	4□11	1□□□-□rese□t	4□.6622	111.04□□
□□□is□ Mo□t□□□	2427□□	4□□1	1□□□-□rese□t	4□.□□□4	111.7111
□e□□e□ D□□□ Mo□t□□□	2440□□	64□□	1□□□-□rese□t	44.□667	111.□□□2
□ivi□□sto□ 12 S□Mo□t□□□	24□0□0	4□6□	1□□□-□rese□t	4□.4□□6	110.6□□
□orris M□□iso□ □ □□ Mo□t□□□	2461□7	474□	1□□□-□rese□t	4□.4□□6	111.6□2□
Re□ □o□□e 2 □□ Mo□t□□□	246□1□	□4□□	1□□□-□rese□t	4□.21□1	10□.2□7□
□ir□i□i□ □it□Mo□t□□□	24□□□7	□770	1□□□-□rese□t	4□.2□2□	111.□4□1
□ est □e□□□ sto□e□Mo□t□□□	24□□□7	66□6	1□□□-□rese□t	44.6□00	111.1000
A□t□ 1 □□□□ □□ □□□ i□□	4□0140	6426	1□□□-□rese□t	4□.772□	111.0□□□
□□□ □□□ □□□ i□□	4□1□40	□0□□	1□□□-□rese□t	44.□21□	10□.06□□
D□□ois□□ □□□ i□□	4□271□	6□□7	1□□□-□rese□t	4□.□□□7	10□.6□□□
□□□e □e□□□ sto□e□□ □□□ i□□	4□□□4□	7□6□	1□□□-□rese□t	44.□61□	110.□□□6
Mor□□ □ □□□□ □□ □□□ i□□	4□6440	67□7	1□□□-□rese□t	4□.□□67	110.□□□□
□i□e□□□e□□ □□□ i□□	4□7260	7174	1□□□-□rese□t	42.□7□7	10□.□642
□e□□□ sto□e M□□ □ ot□□□ □□□ i□□	4□□□0□	6226	1□□□-□rese□t	44.□772	110.6□□□

Table 2. □ □o□ i□□ c□i□ □te st□tio□s □ro□ t□e □oo□ □ et□ or□ □se□ i□ t□is re□ort □ro□ □tt□□□□□ □ □.□ rcc.□ri.e□□coo□□ □□□□

Station name	ID number	Elevation (ft)	Period of record	Latitude	Longitude	Climate Division
□ r□□□□□□□ ree□	4□21□□	6□0□	□□1□1□4□ - □rese□t	44.□7	-10□.64	1
□e□□□ sto□e □ □ □□st □□tr□□ce	4□□□02	6□□2	11□1□1□□□ - □rese□t	44.4□	-110.00	4
□□□□□□□o □i□□ D□□	4□117□	□160	1□ 1□1□0□ - □rese□t	44.□0	-10□.11	4
D□□□i□ R□□c □	4□2□7□	□160	□□1□1□74 - □rese□t	4□.42	-110.1□	2
D□□ois	47271□	6□□□	□□1□1□4□ - □rese□t	4□.□□	-110.6□	□
So□t□ □□ss	4□□□□□	7□40	□□1□1□4□ - □rese□t	42.47	-10□.□0	□

Table 3. □ □o□ i□□ S□ □ T□□ Stati o□s □se□ i□ t□is re□ort □ro□ □tt□□□□□ □ □.□ cc.□rcs.□s□□.□ov□□ote□□□ □o□ i□□□□ □o□ i□□.□t□ □□

Station name	Station ID	Elevation	Period of record	Latitude	Longitude	Basin
□e□rtoot□ □□□e	□26	□□60	10□1□1□7□ - □rese□t	44.□4	-10□.□7	□□□r□s For□ □e□□o□ sto□e
□□□□c□□ □ter	□□0	□7□0	10□1□1□7□ - □rese□t	44.□□	-10□.7□	□ort□ F or□ S□os□o□e
□□rro□□□s □ree□	□7□	□7□0	10□1□1□7□ - □rese□t	4□.7	-10□.67	U□□er □ i□□
□o□□ S□ri□□s	40□	□6□0	10□1□1□□□ - □rese□t	4□.2□	-10□.4□	U□□er □ i□□
Deer □□r□	□2□	□700	□□14□1□□7 - □rese□t	42.□□	-10□.□	□o□o A□ie
□ve□i□□ St□r	472	□200	10□1□1□7□ - □rese□t	44.6□	-10□.7□	□□□r□s For□ □e□□o□ sto□e
G□□si□□t □□ss	□44	□□20	□□□□1□□□ - □rese□t	4□.□□	-10□.□□	Gros □e□tre
□o□□s □ □r□	□2□	10100	10□1□1□7□ - □rese□t	42.□7	-10□.0□	□itt□e□ i□□
□ir□i□	□60	□□□0	10□1□1□7□ - □rese□t	4□.06	-10□.02	Gre□□□□□
□itt□e□ □r□	□□□	□□70	10□1□1□7□ - □rese□t	4□.□	-10□.7□	U□□er □ i□□
M□r□□ette	616	□760	10□1□1□7□ - □rese□t	44.□	-10□.24	□ort□ F or□ S□os□o□e
□□□ □ree□	676	□□7□	10□1□1□7□ - □rese□t	4□.66	-10□.01	U□□er □i□□or□
□□r□er □e□□	6□□	□400	10□1□1□7□ - □rese□t	44.7□	-10□.□1	□e□□o□ sto□e □ e□□□ □ters
So□t□ □□ss	77□	□040	10□1□1□□4 - □rese□t	42.□7	-10□.□4	□o□o A□ie
St. □□□re□ce A□t	7□6	□620	10□1□1□□□ - □rese□t	4□.0□	-10□.17	□itt□e□ i□□
S□□v□□ Ro□□	□07	7120	10□1□1□□6 - □rese□t	44.4□	-110.04	□ort□ F or□ S□os□o□e
Ti□ □er □ree□	□1□	7□□0	10□1□1□□6 - □rese□t	44.0□	-10□.1□	Gre□□□□□
To□ □se□□ □ree□	□26	□700	10□1□1□7□ - □rese□t	42.7	-10□.□	□o□o A□ie
□ o□veri□e	□7□	76□0	10□1□1□7□ - □rese□t	44.□	-10□.66	□□□r□s For□ □e□□o□ sto□e
□o□□ts □e□□	□7□	□□□0	10□1□1□7□ - □rese□t	4□.□□	-10□.□2	So□t□ For□ S□os□o□e